making money online

Also by Antonia Chitty

*Commercial Writing: How to Earn a Living
as a Business Writer*

making money online

antonia chitty
and erica douglas

ROBERT HALE · LONDON

Typeset by e-type, Liverpool
Printed in Great Britain by MPG Books Group,
Bodmin and King's Lynn

Contents

Introduction

Do you see people saying that they are making a great living online, and wish you could too? Right now we are in the midst of a time of change. Traditional manufacturing jobs are on the decline, and even jobs in service industries are harder to find. However there are thousands of *new* ways to earn once you enter the internet. What is more, many of these new ideas for earning can be started part-time, in your spare hours, alongside raising a family or another job.

More and more, successful people are adapting to the new economic climate not just by ditching the idea of a job for life, but also by ceasing to rely on a single job for all their income. This does require a change in the way you think. You need to be open to opportunities and ready to learn. Online earning is only successful for those who persist.

If earning online sounds like something that you would love to do, and you are ready to commit some time and effort to the process, read on. There is hard work ahead of you, but the benefits are immense. You can work from anywhere in the world, at the times of day that suit you.

Making money online is ideal if you are restricted to working limited hours, whether it is because you have another job, a health condition that stops you going out to work or you are at home looking after the family. Beyond that, it can allow you to take time out, travel, have the school holidays off and more, as long as you set up how you earn correctly.

ANYONE CAN DO IT ... WITH SOME EXPERT ADVICE

Whether you view online marketing experts with suspicion or awe, there are lots of people making big claims right now. In order to get the most out of this book, we want to share our experiences with you, as well as those of other internet experts. So, to get started, read how we both learnt, through trial and error, how to earn our livings online.

Our stories

Antonia Chitty is a successful blogger and author. She is the editor of the influential Family Friendly Working blog and is highly influential on Twitter. She has been using the internet to help her earn since 2003, and has tried many different routes to work out her strategy of how to earn online. Antonia explains how she has changed the way she works and found success.

In 2003 I set up a business specializing in PR for baby and child-related products and services. The business grew and I was able to successfully combine it with being mum to one. I took advantage of my second maternity leave to write a book on PR, which meant that after the birth of my second son I diversified into PR training. More books followed and I created a blog to promote one of them called 'Family Friendly Working'.

It was that blog that gave me the first inkling that I would soon unlock a range of new ways to earn.

I have now written fifteen books and created seven websites for my different businesses. I run a daily blog for working parents at Family Friendly Working, and offer tips and advice for mums in business at The Mumpreneur Guide blog. I have run a conference and do other online activities, more of which later.

What is more important than all that activity is that I have learnt how to create a steady monthly income, whether it is term time and I am working hard or school holiday time and I am off having fun with the kids.

In the beginning I simply traded my time for money, providing PR services and charging by the job or by the hour. I had to keep working throughout the school holidays to see my income continue. As my family grew I soon found that with three children rather than one it was getting very hard to find time to make the calls I needed for the PR business to continue on the same basis. I was fortunate enough to come across a well-known internet marketer, Nicola Bird, who at that time was running a site called 'More Than Your Time'. Over eighteen months I changed the way I work. I followed Nicola's advice to get away from just working one-to-one with clients, which was becoming impossible for me, and to focus on ways of using the internet to share the expert advice I could offer without taking up all of my time.

I now get income from a number of streams including:

- The PR agency, which still offers PR, copywriting and, most importantly, blogging services for other businesses. I use a range of freelancers to provide this service and get 99% of my clients online
- My subscription service, www.parentingmagazinecontacts. co.uk, where public relations people and parenting business owners can join to download up-to-date contacts at hundreds of different parenting publications
- My self-published books that I sell via www.mumpreneur-shop.co.uk and www.acebusinesstraining.com. These books are also available on Amazon

- Book royalties from publishers and advances for writing new books
- My features writing on topics where I am an expert and can command above average fees
- The Family Friendly Working and Mumpreneur Guide blogs. I also earn income through banner advertising, directories, sponsored posts, and affiliate schemes like Amazon's when I do product reviews
- Offering online training through www.aceinspire.com and www.becomeamumpreneur.com, with more in the pipeline

If I hadn't joined Nicola's programme I could still be struggling instead of having a range of income streams, some which require very little of my time and others that I can fit in round the kids very happily. As I write this, I am looking at my best year ever for business income, despite only having to work around 20 hours a week.

Erica Douglas is a leading blogger who's been making a part-time income online since 2007. She combines a full-time university degree with earning a full-time income online – working only a few hours a week. She's a promoter of multiple streams of income and passive income business models. She had no previous business experience, proving that anyone can make an income online with a bit of hard work. Erica tells her story:

In 2009 I was working part-time as a waitress, a job I enjoyed but that was physically demanding. Events that year meant I had to resign, leaving me with very little personal income.

A few months later I found myself well enough to seek work again. I attended the Job Centre every week only to be disheartened to find that the recession meant that opportunities were limited. With every week that passed and every visit to the Job Centre I felt more and more depressed and my self-esteem was suffering.

I had been trying to make a go of things online but the small amount of income I was earning via my blog wasn't really enough. In October 2009 my husband told me to stop looking for a job. He promised that he'd make up the difference in overtime: we needed about £200–300 per month to cover the gap.

I took his advice and, well, he never had to do any overtime. My husband is a sensible guy. He figured that by taking away the barriers it really put me under (good) pressure to follow my passion and as soon as I started taking it seriously I started earning an income.

I 'work' for around fifteen hours a week now on various things but predominantly my income comes from training businesswomen how to use the internet more effectively. I chose that niche as it is something I am hugely passionate about but there are a ton of different niches out there. My target in the first six months of 2010 was to exceed my waitressing income of £400–500 per month. My target by the end of 2010 was to earn more than £1,000 per month, working just ten hours a week (I am not lazy, I am studying full-time too!).

Come December 2010, I exceeded my target. I know it is not a huge amount (I am not rich, yet!) but it was a big milestone. My target for 2011 is to earn a 'full-time wage on part-time hours' and I calculate that as £1,500 per month before tax. As I write this I currently earn around £2,000 per month.

THE 'MAKING MONEY' MINDSET

Throughout this book we won't just be teaching you practical techniques for online earning, though there are plenty of those. We will be asking you to change the way you think, indeed to forget everything you have been taught about work and earning money. The way you think is called a 'mindset' and later on you can read about developing a helpful mindset to make earning easier.

If you want to start earning online, you will soon find other people making dismissive comments. Ignore the people who say it is impossible to 'have it all'. The sad truth is that some people do not want to see you succeed because it calls into question the decisions they have made and continue to make. Let them make the decisions for themselves and you can concentrate on making great decisions for yourself.

Coach Allison Marlowe says:

> I have been on my own personal development journey for around 15 years. Every now and then I take a quantum leap. I do not worry any more about the money: my experience is when I step up, I just go with it. I have an unwritten rule that when I do invest big, I make that money back within a couple of months. I paid £15,000 to join a group and made £18,000 back within a couple of months. The knowledge that I have is valuable to other people. I know it inside out, upside down. People are buying me, buying my time, buying my expertise. Once you can get your head round the fact that what you know is not known to everybody, it is a gift and other people do value it. I believe that I deserve to ask for money in return for that. I played small and it really does not work. When I put my prices up, more people recommend me.

YOUR GOALS

Before you start earning online, get clear in your own mind why you are doing this and what you want to achieve. This will make it easier for you to stay on track and concentrate on activities that get you closer to your goal.

Ask yourself, 'What do I want?' You could be looking for a bit of spare cash that just means you have enough money for treats or to avoid going overdrawn. You might be looking for a part-time income instead of getting a job, or so you can cut down your hours. Alternatively, you might be studying or caring for family and in need of a flexible income that allows you to work around your regular commitments. Maybe, like us, you have the goal of earning a full-time income on part-time hours.

We are living proof that this can be done and we want to share that with you. All the things you will learn in this book are concepts and strategies that we use day in, day out to make four figures a month on just ten or twenty hours' work a week.

We are not writing about any sort of 'get rich quick' scheme. If you need a sum of money right now then please do a boot sale or look for a job. What you will learn from this book is long-term strategy, not a 'make £1,000 in 24 hours' scam.

If you have had enough of being beholden to bosses, juggling childcare, having no spare cash, feeling that you are not contributing financially or struggling with debt then read on because what we have to say could change your life.

LIFE CHANGE STARTS HERE

We have three essential concepts that we want you to understand before moving on to the rest of the book. Get these ideas right and you will have taken the first step to changing the way you earn so it can be done alongside other commitments.

Concept 1: multiple streams of income

The first concept that will change the way you think about earning is **multiple streams of income** – there is lots to this topic, which will become evident as you read through the book but let's start with a short explanation.

Think about what is happening in the world right now. Business owners are going out of business and employees are being made redundant left, right and centre. For these people that business or that job was their sole source of income. Does the idea that your entire life is dependent on one source of income make you feel uncomfortable? You can end up in dire straits through no fault of your own, such as when the recession took hold. Gone are the days when jobs were for life and large establishments like Woolworths could never go down. We do not want to scaremonger, far from it, but times have changed and it is time we changed with them.

Imagine this alternative scenario: Sharon worked on the till at Woolies twenty hours a week, but she also has a number of online incomes. She writes a parenting blog that earns her £300 a month in advertising. She does some freelance writing for £150 per month. Sharon's also just launched an eBook from a blog in a niche area which earns £75 a month and she's in the process of launching an eCourse. Woolies go bust in the recession and what does Sharon do? Sharon cuts back and lives off her other incomes. She spends her free time creating that eCourse which grows to earn her around £300 a month and she invested her redundancy money in another business opportunity which she hopes will be a big success.

No matter which of Sharon's incomes disappears she has others on which to rely, and it is highly unlikely that all her incomes will dry up at the same time. This is the theory behind multiple streams of income.

What does this mean for you?

It means you do not need one big idea or lots of investment to cease being reliant on an employer. If you are a business owner it takes a lot of the risk out of being an entrepreneur as, instead of relying on one idea or one market, you have a number of enterprises.

This might sound like a big commitment, but in this book we explain how you can build up an online income incrementally while still working or alongside your other commitments. This is exactly what we have done: we have built our incomes up gradually to a point where our 'work' is flexible and our incomes are multiple.

What do you think of this concept?

Concept 2: passive income

So, has the concept about multiple income streams got you thinking? You might be thinking, 'Great, when can I start?' or you might be wondering just how you find time to generate several different ways of earning when right now you are struggling with just one. Concept two, **passive income**, is going to stop you worrying right now.

What is passive income?

Different people have a slightly different definition as to what constitutes passive income. For us it is income that comes from a source that does not require ongoing work. So interest from your ISA would be classed as passive income, as would appreciation of your valuables. Our passive incomes include affiliate marketing income, eBooks, eCourses, sidebar advertising and membership subscriptions. All of these incomes do not require a time commitment every day.

These incomes continue to flow regardless of your input. It is worth investing time upfront to create this sort of ongoing income. As examples, we have written books and created eCourses and directories, in the knowledge that our time invested upfront will create an ongoing passive income.

Passive income is one reason why the 'rich always get richer' or why 'money goes to money'. With the internet you too have the opportunity to create these passive incomes for yourself.

What passive incomes do you currently have? How can you maximize your passive income? Think of ways online and offline: you will get lots of ideas as you work through this book.

Concept 3: leveraging your time

Concept three will help you make the most of whatever time you have, whether it is a few hours at evenings and weekends, or ninety minutes each day while your toddler naps. Leverage your time by starting to move away from selling your time by the hour. You can only go so far when you are selling your time as you only have so much time to sell!

Leverage your time by finding someone you can pay to do activities for less than the income they generate. If you are setting up an online shop and have hundreds of products to load onto the shop, it will be more cost effective to find someone else to do this while you get on with promoting the store. If you have a business and are doing your own accounts you could work more effectively by finding a bookkeeper and getting on with using your skills where they are most effective.

There are many more ways to leverage your time. If you are a coach, for example, you might offer group coaching where you can coach a number of people at once rather than simply working one to one. If you own a business, franchising will move you on from 'doing it all' to having a number of other people who are all contributing to your income.

Leverage your products and knowledge

If you have extensive knowledge on a topic you can leverage your time by creating an eBook. You write the book once, but it can be sold many times over without further commitment from you. Your expertise could also be used to create an eCourse that can be delivered automatically.

Keep thinking of ways to leverage what you already have in a way that can earn you a passive income.

Leverage your income

Invest some of the income you make into training and other business ideas. Always stay one step ahead. Get into the habit of investing a percentage of your income into training and new ventures. We always find training to be money well spent. We can learn what we need to maximize our earnings in the future.

Sometimes the first investment is the hardest because that's coming direct from your own pocket.

WHAT NEXT?

So, now you know how we have created our own flexible incomes. Plus, you have started to learn about three essential concepts that will allow you to earn online in a flexible way. Now it is time to get stuck into learning about the practical techniques you will need to earn your first few pounds online.

1 Finding Your Niche

WHY HAVE A NICHE?

You might be raring to go, all ready to find ways to make money online, but first I am going to ask you a question. Why should people buy from you? Unless you have something to offer that is unique and different, any attempts to make money online are going to be largely wasted as you struggle to get yourself noticed in crowded marketplaces. If you can find a niche with little competition and become known as the person to go to for relevant information, products and services you will be in a strong position to make money.

Helen Lindop has spent a number of years researching niches for entrepreneurs. She explains why a niche is a good idea:

> You do not have the time or the money to reach out to a wide range of buyers, so you need your promotional activities to be focused in one place. 'Niching' can be scary, though. It is tempting to try to be all things to all people because you do not want to lose customers. The trouble with this is that if you do not know exactly who your customers are, you can't go to the places they hang out. And you can't explain to them that you have got a fab new widget that will solve a pressing problem of theirs. Having a niche does not mean you have to turn other people away. Your niche is the focus of your promotional efforts rather than a strict rule about who you can sell to. Here's another big advantage: if you have got a

niche, you can become an expert in your chosen area much faster than you would otherwise. Given the choice, wouldn't you go to the expert first?

Case Study: Helen Lindop of Business Plus Baby

www.businessplusbaby.com

It took Helen Lindop eight years to find her niche, and she's now working on monetizing it. Read her journey:

I had been a freelance IT trainer for a few years in 2002. Changes in the IT industry at that time meant it was getting harder to find training work. When I saw a couple of training companies I had freelanced for go bust I knew it was time to add another string to my bow. Coaching was not widely known in the UK then, but I read about it in a magazine and liked the idea of becoming a coach. I also felt it would complement my training experience, so I signed up for a three year part-time coach training course.

Most of the tutors on my course told me how important it was to pick a niche. But they didn't fully explain how to do it, other than to pick one where I had some interest and experience. This is a good place to start, but I was missing something.

I picked 'solopreneurs' as my niche, one-person businesses. I knew the problems this group faced very well – ups and downs in workload and cashflow, being let down by clients, struggling to stay motivated and the Government taking an outrageous amount of tax out of your pay packet.

I have always been fascinated by tiny businesses, the type where someone says 'Right, I am sick of being a cog in someone else's machine, I am going to do my own thing instead'. So I had both experience and a passion for this niche.

My problem was that this was actually several niches, rather than just the one. An IT engineer working on 3 month contracts was entirely different from a self-employed complementary therapist, for example. Yes, they had similar problems, but they lived in different worlds, thought in different ways and hung around with different people. Self-employment wasn't bringing them together at all.

If I had picked IT contractors or complementary therapists or journalists or one (wo)man craft businesses or plumbers I might have got somewhere.

After four years of trying to run my freelance IT training business, my fledgling coaching business and do my coaching studies all at the same time I realised I needed to change my approach. A permanent job came up in my perfect location that matched my IT training experience amazingly well. By that time a steady pay cheque really appealed to me so I took the job.

A couple of years after that I was a new mum who was dreading returning to my job after my maternity leave ended. I knew self-employment could be an option but didn't know where to start. And it took months to find the information I needed. If I was struggling to get started with my experience as a freelance, I knew mums who had known nothing but employment would be even worse off.

So I started a new website for solopreneurs, but this time my approach was totally different. Previously my starting point was 'I want to coach people'. This time my starting point was a well-defined group of people facing a specific challenge: new mums starting out in business. The solution to their problems could be coaching but it could also be training, a workshop, a book, an e-course or something I had not yet thought of. I was drawn mainly towards online courses as, after six years of freelancing, I had had enough of trading my time for money!

This time I would let the niche tell me what it wanted, instead of assuming that coaching was the solution. That was my approach to businessplusbaby.com.

For over a year I thought my niche was mums with very young children who were thinking of starting family-friendly businesses. Then I surveyed my readers and found most had children aged from three to five years and were in the first year of running their businesses. That was just the average – I also had readers who had been in business over three years and had children aged five to eighteen-plus. To my surprise only a tiny number of my readers had babies and hadn't yet launched their businesses. That showed me just how important it is to listen to my audience!

Fortunately it is much easier to widen a niche that's too narrow than it is to narrow one that's too wide. I changed my focus, and my tag line, from 'starting a business as mum to a baby or toddler' to 'growing a business around a young family'. I haven't lost any readers; it is early days so far but the hits on my website are actually going up.

If I could go back and speak to myself in 2002 I'd tell myself to find a group of people that I find truly fascinating, get to know them incredibly well and then work out what I can do to help them. This is the opposite of what I actually did when I signed up for my coaching course.

HOW TO FIND A NICHE

Now, down to the nuts and bolts of finding a niche. Your first thought when looking into making money online may be to find a nice big niche with lots of searches, something like 'online dating' or 'weight loss', but it can be really hard to make an impact in this sort of crowded market, however many people there are searching. If you think of your own behaviour when searching online, do you often look beyond the first page of search engine results? You need to find a focused niche where you can achieve a listing on the first page in search engine results in order for a site to make you money, ideally where you are within the first three results.

In order to do this you need to do keyword research. Once you have a broad idea of an area that you might focus on, start looking at the keywords potential customers might search on. Enter these into something like the Google Keyword Tool. Google 'free keyword tool for adwords' or paste this into your browser: https://adwords.google.com/select/KeywordToolExternal

It will come up with a range of suggestions for similar keywords, phrases that include your keywords and more. Pick a phrase, drill down by adding in further words to make your phrase more specific, and explore similar phrases with slightly different wording. Assess the number of searches and the degree of competition as indicated by the Keyword Tool. You are looking for phrases with a moderate search volume, at least several thousand per month and with as little competition as possible. If your phrase relates to something you can supply globally look at the global searches, if not, look at the local searches.

This is not quite as simple as it seems: search volumes can differ depending on whether you are logged in or logged out of the Google tool. The Keyword Tool does not show search volumes. It shows 'the approximate 12-month average of user queries for the keyword on Google.co.uk and the Google Search Network', which can lead to inflated search volumes, and data based on searches a few months ago. So, alongside using the Keyword Tool, search on Google and see what 'autocomplete' terms appear. For example, if you are searching for 'Keep calm and ...' you will find that when you type just those three words into a Google search box, it suggests firstly 'Keep Calm and Carry On', but, at the time of writing, this is swiftly followed by 'Keep Calm and Be Reem', a catchphrase from *The Only Way is Essex* TV show. This phrase wouldn't have appeared in the top search terms even a few months earlier. Google Autocomplete gives different results on the Google web search page, which is based on search volumes over a number of months to the Google news search page, which is based on current search terms. By checking your possible phrases in all these places you can assess whether you have a phrase worth optimizing for.

Once you have some ideas for key phrases surrounding your potential niche, type them into a range of different search engines. How many web pages appear when you search? Examine the top ranking sites on the first page of results. Check out some of the lower ranking pages and see what they might be missing.

Tools to help with niche research

There are various online tools to help you with researching keywords and niches. Starting very simply, look at Rob Millard's Keyword Expander, http://www.rob-millard.com/keyword-expander, which helps you drill down from keywords and phrases and check trends for use in Google searches over the years. You can also download further tools including Micro Niche Finder, http://www.micronichefinder.com, and Market Samurai, http://www.marketsamurai.com, which claim to help you find untapped niches.

A person-centred approach

Helen Lindop advises,

The trick is to find a group of people that a) already hang out together and b) really want something that you have (or can get for them). Why? Well it is a lot easier to find your customers and talk to them as a group if they are already meeting up, reading the same websites or buying the same magazines.

Plus it is easier to sell to them if you have a solution to one of their problems than if you think you have got something they might like.

MONEY-MAKING NICHES

Once you have some ideas for a niche focused on certain key phrases, assess whether it is one that will have the potential to make you money. An easy-to-monetize niche is one that is

- product-focused
- full of buyers with a reasonable amount of disposable income
- under-serviced
- already making money for other people

Case study: Chrissie Slade of Gorgeous Guineas

www.gorgeousguineas.co.uk

Chrissie Slade has been in business for 7 years, offering aromatherapy skincare products for guinea pigs. This is the perfect example of a niche business, and here you can read just how Chrissie got started.

It was a guinea pig called Florence who started my business journey. I had kept guinea pigs since childhood, but I had no idea that you could adopt guinea pigs until I saw Florence advertised in a local paper. I contacted Karen who runs a guinea pig rescue, we got chatting, and I adopted Florence. I also offered to foster some guinea pigs for Karen and, when I found she didn't have a website, offered to set that up too.

Six weeks later Karen took in 17 guinea pigs at once, and she told me that they had some really bad skin problems. Conventional treatment from the vet wasn't making an impact either. I had had a long term interest in aromatherapy and had qualified as an aromatherapist some years earlier. My main interest was in developing products, so I offered to see if I could develop something to help the guinea pigs. I had had success with human skin problems and was confident I could come up with similar remedies on a guinea pig scale.

There were some things I had to take into account. Guinea pigs are much smaller than humans so I could only use very tiny amounts of essential oils, and because of the fact that they are covered with hair, I focussed on lotions which would absorb quickly without leaving a greasy residue, and shampoos to remove scurf.

Once I found that the products worked well on 17 guinea pigs it seemed like it would be fun to start a small business alongside my full time job in corporate project management. It took about a year for me to research and develop the products to get Gorgeous Guineas off the ground, and then another year went by. I was then offered the chance to go part time: I leapt at the opportunity to cut down to three days at work and to spend more time developing a bigger range of products.

Finally, with the business and website up and running, I took the plunge and quit the corporate world. I now work full time on Gorgeous Guineas, but also enjoy the freedom to nip out and do things like getting my hair cut and going to the vets when I need to. I am so much happier working for myself.

The key element to my success started when I got the idea of working with other guinea pig rescue centres. I send them sample products which they can offer to people who adopt guinea pigs in their care, some of whom need rehoming just because they have skin problems. You can see little clusters of customers building up in the areas where I have done this. I partner with likeminded online stores who can sell my products. I also have an overseas distributor in the Netherlands, and am looking for distributors in other countries.

I promote Gorgeous Guineas on Facebook and Twitter, I send out newsletters twice a month and have a blog. All these help me find the people who need my product, alongside great search engine results for key words related to guinea pig skin conditions.

You must have a niche. I could be an aromatherapist, but there are 50 or more in my town. Why would anyone come to me? With my niche I have customers from across the globe who seek me out online.

If you are inspired by Chrissie's story she has some guidance for anyone looking to start a niche business:

- Start with something you know about. I had my aromatherapy diploma and lots of experience in looking after guinea pigs
- Make sure you are passionate about your topic. Passion will keep you motivated, and if you are not passionate it shows
- Get coaching or mentoring: I use Nick Williams of www.inspired-entrepreneur.com. This can help you stay passionate and inspired and develop a sound business model
- Always look for new inspiration in your niche: for me new oils can help me develop new products
- Creating your site is not hard: blog software and PayPal buttons make it straightforward for non-technical people
- Do not, however, struggle over tedious jobs. I have used freelancers that I have found through Elance to create my shopping cart, do design work and even create spreadsheets of what I have sold
- Finally, never compromise on the quality of what you offer

NICHE MARKETING

Once you have your niche, you need to consider how you will raise your profile in this area, find people who are interested, get them to your site or online store and make sales. Niche marketing is all about focusing your communications about your product or service towards a well-defined group of people. You can further refine your niche by looking at price range, quality and demographic data: consider the age, gender and location of the people in your niche.

Research for niche marketing

Helen Lindop has some good advice about developing your profile in a niche area:

> Tell everyone you know about your niche, send mailings to the places where your niche gets together, set up a Facebook page: all good steps, but do not stop there. Now go and immerse yourself in that community. Get to know what is on their minds, where they shop, what they really want from a product or service like yours. Tell them what you are doing and ask what they think. If your product or service is slightly off track, this is where you will be able to realign it. Plus, you will become the person this community go to when they need that product or service.

BEYOND NICHE

Alongside all this research, make sure that the niche you pick is something that you can be interested in, even passionate about. Read Nick Williams' case study below, to find out why:

Case study: Nick Williams of Inspired Entrepreneur

www.inspired-entrepreneur.com

Nick Williams is an author, coach, motivational speaker and co-founder of Inspired Entrepreneur. In his 20s, he worked selling office equipment, and succumbed to what he now calls the 'Protestant work ethic' – work hard, make sacrifices in order to become successful. Nick moved job roles and, at about the same time, came across Alternatives, an organization running personal growth events in London, which had a profound effect on his life. He says, 'I stopped drinking and became more conscious – I was now willing to feel my emotions instead of masking them under alcohol'. He knew he wanted to change direction, but was in turmoil and ended up working for three more years before he summoned up the courage to quit. At that time he was a highly driven, top sales performer, selling computers globally and winning numerous sales trips to exotic places. However, it dawned on him that he'd spent his whole life trying to show everyone that he wasn't a failure.

He didn't transform his life overnight, though. Nick took time out to travel. He says it was the most exciting yet painful of times: 'I travelled around America, New Zealand, Australia, Singapore and Thailand, had a holiday romance and fell in love. I wanted to be far away from home. I thought to myself: "Yeah, I'm ok to claim my own independence, my own identity, and stand on my own two feet without a company behind me".' However, on his return Nick hit rock bottom. He came back to the UK with no income; he felt like a failure and signed on to the dole. Feeling lost, unloved and scared, this was to be the turning point that would lead Nick to break free: 'I was sitting on the fence questioning whether I wanted to live or die', says Nick. 'I chose to make a commitment to life rather than to death – and start living. So in November 1990, I came off the dole and with no entrepreneurial role models from my family, started my first company. I began to put myself out into the world as a trainer and seminar promoter.'

Nick worked through his own journey of self-development, and at the same time worked on projects with many of the leading lights of the personal development world. The next breakthrough for Nick was when he realized how much he had learned from organizing talks, but that he was also 'hiding out', and it was time to really 'show up'. He wanted to be the one giving the talks rather than organizing them. He devoted his energy to developing his own career in speaking, writing, educating and broadcasting. Since then, Nick's book, *The Work We Were Born To Do*, became an international bestseller and put his name on the global map. His message that work should involve joy, and that you can earn a living from doing what you love, has resonated globally. From there, Nick has carved out a name for himself as a public speaker, coach, writer, event organizer for other leaders, and a collaborator. He has so far been invited to speak in sixteen countries, and has written six books with more on their way.

Nick says:

I've been down the conventional career path, selling computers. I worked a lot for the money, not for the love. I didn't find it rewarding and fulfilling. I explored what I thought I could be interested in, personal growth, psychology. I struggled for 3 years of soul searching. Part of me knew where I wanted to go and part of me was terrified to change. I got to the place where it was too painful not to change. I had some real low times and some challenging times where I thought I had gone mad. For me it was about unearthing what I really wanted to do, and this is what I now share. Each of us has unique gifts and talents, we are fulfilled when we are exercising our strengths.

The internet plays a huge role in my business. I set up Inspired Entrepreneur around six years ago, and soon realized how much the world had changed. I thought, 'I've got to get my head round the internet.' We have developed a sophisticated platform so people can learn and interact. If you want to make money online, the first thing to do is figure out what difference you want to make. The website and social media are just the vehicles to do that. Some people can do very well simply following a trend, thinking 'Where's the money?' but it's not fulfilling. I've taken the longer route and for me it is worth it. It takes time to build a following, build a tribe, build a reputation and do it with integrity. It is a worthwhile route. I have a lot of respect and people who will spread the word. I'm teaching people how they can pioneer in their own lives: I'm a servant teacher.

If you want to create an online income and have passion for what you do, Nick advises,

Really become a human being. I go to so many websites and see professional services but not the person behind it. Create an emotional connection with people before you ask them to spend money with you. I give away a lot for free and in doing that I create bonds. I'm honest, authentic; people can see me for real. That leads to building a tribe, a group of people who in essence you set out to serve. Seth Godin's book, *Tribes*, had a profound impact on me. I've built my tribe over the last 5–6 years, we have an email list of around 23,000 people, and all my business comes from those people.

If you want to build your own tribe, Nick advises,

Give a gift to start with. People can tell the difference between a gift and sales or marketing. Even if you never spend money with me I would love to help you. I live a spiritual mission to contribute to people. People want to come back and spend money on what I want to do. I don't want to work for pay, I want to be paid for my work. It is a different approach, one that encourages people to have their gift and their artistry in life. You work for the love but you are willing to be paid for what you love doing. If you are going to have an internet business, you need to convey why you're doing what you're doing. I always want to know this: why are you doing this, beyond making money? Everyone's blog or website needs to convey the bigger why. If people see you have a bigger sense of purpose, paradoxically they are more likely to spend money.

Nick has some advice on understanding success. He says,

You can measure your success. Ask yourself, do I feel aligned in what I am doing? Secondly, are you creating ripples, getting feedback, do people tell you they like what you are doing? Thirdly, do people trust you, have you conveyed yourself so people want to spend money? It shows again that you're having an impact. Things like getting referrals, creating ripples, are wonderful. When you do a good job people will recommend you. Today more than ever people believe personal recommendation. I tend not to buy anything cold myself today. Be transparent: if you say one thing but do something else it will come out. Even if you make a mistake be open. My business is helping people find their own personal brilliance. Build a business around what you are thrilled to do every day. Raise your sights rather than lower them. Today to succeed, show up with the best of you, your own passion, love and care.

TAKING ACTION

Niche marketing activity is similar to any sort of marketing. If right now you think 'I know nothing about marketing', that's fine. Over the next two chapters we will guide you step by step through how to develop your online profile. What you need to do is create a plan of action. Any marketing activities, and this includes using social media, will only succeed if you can do them regularly. As you go through this book make a list of the different things you can do to spread the word about what you offer and book in fifteen minutes or more each day to do one thing towards raising your profile.

Evaluate what is working: track the number of hits you get to your site using Google Analytics. Work out where people come from and what actions they take when they visit your site. You will then begin to learn what marketing works well for you.

Read more about raising your profile, finding fans and spreading the word in Chapter 3, Building Your Profile as an Expert and Finding Followers.

SUMMING UP: KEY FACTORS TO ASSESS YOUR POTENTIAL NICHE

Consider what you want to sell through your niche: affiliate products, your own products or services, and then review the following factors:

- Number of searches both globally and in your locality
- Competition on search terms
- The number of other web pages that appear when you search on the chosen terms
- Whether you have a niche that ties in to a product
- Whether you have a niche that relates to a product with a good price or an affiliate scheme with good rates

- How the niche ties in with your own skills
- Whether you have a niche that you can remain interested in
- Whether you have a niche to which you have lots to contribute
- Whether the niche is likely to have buyers with disposable income – keen hobbyists for example
- Whether other people appear to be making money in this niche (remembering to avoid too much competition)

No niche is likely to meet all these criteria but the more you can tick off the better.

2 Starting a Blog

Now you understand a bit more about finding a niche, it is time to learn about blogging. Creating and 'maintaining' a blog is a relatively simple process. It is a case of completing a number of tasks well, over and over again. Blogging is very much about compound effort. For example, one blog post might attract five people from search engines. Multiply that by 100 posts and you are up to 500 readers a day, and that's just search engine traffic! Different niches have different traffic levels so it is difficult to say what is a good amount of traffic. As long as your traffic is constantly increasing then you can take comfort in the fact that you are doing something right.

Traffic is the key to success when we are talking about making money from blogging. Whether you are planning to create a professional platform from which to launch a freelance career or you have got a niche idea that could grow into information products like eBooks and eCourses, blogging is a great way to start building the traffic you need so that you can start to make money online. The point of blogging is for people to become aware of your content and to consume it. You may want traffic so that you can become influential and attract opportunities such as speaking engagements and consulting work. You may wish to leverage your audience to get a book deal, or maybe you just wish to monetize your site with ads. Whatever your goal, getting traffic to your blog is where it all starts.

Read on to find out the basics of blogging and how a blog can become a money-maker.

BLOGGING BASICS

What is a blog?

A blog is a type of website. The word 'blog' is a derivative from its initial title 'web log' which describes it perfectly, a log on the web. The first ever blogs were developed in the early 90s and since then blogging has become a worldwide phenomenon. Nowadays there are millions of blogs on every topic you can think of and some bloggers make up to seven figures a year, from monetizing their blogs as well as launching products, and speaking and freelance careers.

Many people often wonder what makes a blog different from a standard website. On a blog the content is updated regularly with daily or weekly entries. These entries are called 'posts'; the latest posts appear nearest the top of the homepage and work backwards in date order down the page. Older posts are then archived and a tagging system is used to help readers find older content that is relevant to them. A blog can be maintained and updated by one person or a team of writers.

Blogs are also different to websites in that they are interactive. Readers can leave comments on the blog posts, allowing a two-way interaction between reader and publisher.

Blogs can simply be online diaries, or they can be focused on a specific topic such as a hobby or business. Tightly focused blogs on a specific topic are often called niche websites and this type of site is much easier to monetize than a very general blog covering a wide range of sub-topics. For example, a blog on all aspects of parenting would need a more specific niche. Could it become a blog on natural parenting, or a review site for baby equipment?

Blogs are great money-makers as search engines love the continuous fresh content, which means that blogs rank really well in search engine results, much better than an average website. Therefore, blogs receive an above average amount of traffic. Couple this with the relaxed style and interactivity of most blogs and it is a winning combination for both attracting traffic and turning that traffic into loyal readers and consumers of your content, who will hopefully then become consumers of your products and services.

The traffic to your blog can be monetized on two levels, through advertising and through selling products and services, but we will come back to that a bit later in the book. First, read on to get clear about the basics of a successful blog.

Why blog?

There are many different motivations to blogging. The main two are:

For pleasure: humans have always enjoyed the process of log keeping or journal writing; blogging just uses internet technology to do this in a 21st century way. Many people write blogs for pure enjoyment; they can be diaries of their lives or a record of their knowledge on a specific topic.

For business: other people blog to earn money or raise the profile of their business. Blogs with the specific purpose of earning money will occupy very tight niches, provide high quality information and the owners will be focused on the pursuit of monetizing the traffic. Sites like these can be monetized by selling products, advertising and affiliate marketing.

A new and developing trend is that of the 'business blog'. This is a blog that has posts based on topics relating to the business. Business blogs are used to increase customer loyalty, to further cement the brand, as a communication tool and to help potential customers find the business via search engines.

Here's what social media expert Chris Brogan has to say on business blogs:

Blogging is a great way to provide useful information to your potential community about your products and services. Websites with static data rarely encourage return visits, if you think about how sales work, that's the equivalent of someone walking by your shop windows, not seeing something that immediately catches their fancy, and then they wander off forever. Instead, having a blog puts new information and possible offers in front of that passer-by every time you update.

Blogging also adds organic search results to the web so that people who use Google or Bing to find you might catch up on a post of yours and wander into your shop for more information. Blogs have very high authority ratings in services like Google, and blogging software like WordPress really ups the potential search engine optimization (SEO) value of your site. Even if you do not choose to write daily updates (weekly or twice a month is how some do it), this is a great way to add value.

Blogging platforms

In terms of hosting, blogs are split into two main types, hosted or self-hosted. A hosted blog is one that is hosted on a parent site. These blogs are usually free but you never really own your space. The other type is self-hosted, where you buy a domain name and sign up for your own server space with a hosting company. This means that you own full rights to the space. Other advantages include being able to advertise freely and customize your blog's interface (the bit the reader sees).

Blogger

The first type of blog is one that uses a site like Blogger. This is the free and easy way to set up a blog. You simply sign up for an account, choose one of the ready-made templates and start writing. This is the way in which many people start out initially. The barriers of entry are very low and you really need no technical knowledge whatsoever.

Leading parenting blogger and social media consultant Tara Cain (www.stickyfingers1.blogspot.com) says, 'Blogger has worked perfectly for me. I have been able to customise it as much as I wanted and find it super easy to use. I am sure there are lots of advantages to having a self-hosted blog, but I haven't seen any which make me want to make the change.'

The disadvantages as stated are that you do not own the space and could hypothetically have your blog shut down at any time. There are also limitations to customizing the themes and advertising.

Michelle Mitton of www.scribbit.blogspot.com says:

Blogger is perfect for the beginning and intermediate blogger in that it is user-friendly and has most of the needed features built-in, requiring next to no coding experience to manipulate and customize. Once a blogger has become more tech-savvy and conscious of the variety of platforms available and starts to notice how much Wordpress has to offer it becomes pretty tempting to expand your blogging experience by migrating to a platform that allows you to do so much customization and optimization for the search engines.

It is kind of like owning a basic 1967 Chevy Impala. The most popular car ever sold and if that's the only car you had ever saw in your town you'd think it the most wonderful thing for getting you from point A to point B. But once you got out on the road and started to notice all the other fancier cars and how individualized they all were you might start to get a little impatient that you do not have things like power windows, anti-lock brakes, Bose sound, built-in GPS or the other luxuries of the road. Blogger is a very sturdy, very popular, very basic Chevy Impala.

Typepad

Typepad is another blog hosting service where you can get a .typepad.com, such as Joesblog.typepad.com, domain and start blogging very quickly. It charges a small monthly fee. Linda Jones, journalist and CEO of Passionate Media, says:

I first started blogging through the company Shiny Media and the platform they used was Typepad. Although the rate for blogging was low, I learned so much about the system that I felt it would be worth my while to use it elsewhere. I had first blogged with Blogger in 2005/6 but found Typepad much easier, with an appearance I preferred. I am not the most technical of people but Typepad provided excellent tips and hints on how to blog effectively. I appreciated the way it was so easy to link to other blogs, building a community and raising awareness about my blog which at that time was to help multiple birth families [those with twins, triplets etc.].

Over the years Typepad has evolved and I have remained loyal because I find the layout and features so straightforward to navigate. These days I also work with companies and organizations to power their blogs and I do this through Typepad too. It can be very quick to set up an impressive-looking blog with Typepad and the SEO potential is also a factor. I have considered switching to Wordpress and may look at that again, following pointers from other bloggers, but up to now I have always had an 'if it ain't broke, do not fix it' mentality where blogging is concerned.

WordPress

WordPress is a blog publishing platform. Via WordPress.org, you can purchase your own domain and hosting and then install WordPress, which is the most simple platform for publishing a blog. There are thousands of free templates available that can be further customized, giving the publisher complete control over the look of his or her blog. Other features include 'plug-ins', which are add-ons to enhance the performance of your blog. Some of the most popular plug-ins help bloggers with SEO (search engine optimization), comment moderation and dealing with spam comments. Cathy James of www.nurturestore.co.uk says, 'I have been on self-hosted wordpress from the start. I wanted to have more freedom to run the blog how I wanted and this seemed the best option.' WordPress also has a hosted option at www.WordPress.com. It is important not to get the two options confused. WordPress. com is similar to Blogger but with more customization tools. Note that WordPress.com has strict policies on advertising and any blog that you do not own the rights to is in danger of being shut down at any time.

In terms of monetizing your site the best option is without a doubt your own domain and the WordPress.org publishing platform. Do not worry if you already have a blogspot blog or a WordPress.com site: the content can be switched over onto your new domain.

SETTING UP YOUR BLOG

Choosing a name and URL

Before choosing a name for your blog, make sure you have done your keyword research. See Chapter 1 to remind yourself about this.

The name and URL (web address) of your blog should be very similar and where possible exactly the same. Aim to get the .com and if possible the localized URL too. If you are in the UK then this would be the .co.uk. Avoid using complicated spellings, hyphens and ensure that your URL is no longer than thirty-five characters. Ensure that your title as a URL does not throw up any odd word combinations. For example:

'Experts Exchange' becomes www.expertsexchange.com
Not quite hitting the right professional note! Get a few people
to check over your blog title and URL to make sure it conveys
the message you want it to. Finally, once you are completely satisfied purchase your domain name from a domain name broker
like 123-reg, 1and1 or GoDaddy.

If you already have a blog but decide on a new name or
domain name, remember that you can transfer the content from
one domain to another but all your hard work in building up
authority with search engines and links will be lost, so better to
get it right first time.

Blog features

Once you have your domain name and have decided which blog
provider to go with, you need to familiarize yourself with some
different blog features. Read on to understand more about these
and to get to grips with which features are critical if you want
your blog to make money.

Sidebar

Most blogs have a sidebar, usually to the left or right of the
screen, which is used for navigation around the site, promotional
material and advertising. The top of the sidebar is the most
important place on your site to add a 'call to action'. In this spot
there is usually a picture and a short 'about me' sentence. If the
blog is going to be commercial then you may want to include a
free resource on offer for signing up to an email list. We will
discuss email lists later on in this book.

Some bloggers will use the remaining 'above the fold' part of
the sidebar (the section showing before the reader has to scroll)
for banner or text link advertising. It is normal to have a search
bar, archives and categories to help the reader navigate your blog.

Finally, the sidebar will usually feature links to Twitter, Facebook and Flickr accounts along with badges to any other groups the blogger is involved with. If the blog is a business blog then a banner ad leading to the shop or business website is also recommended. Put the most important information and calls to action above the fold.

Pages

The pages of a blog are static. This means that they do not move with the usual chronological flow of the blog posts. The pages can usually be found along the top of the blog just below the header or in one of the sidebars. Below are the most common types of pages.

ABOUT

Almost all blogs will have an 'about me' page, which will be a piece introducing the writer(s) and explaining the purpose of the blog. A picture (or several) along with links to a few articles is also normal. This page is important as it gives your readers a place to go to get a very quick introduction to who you are and what you do. Be sure to keep this page updated with relevant information and up-to-date pictures and links. Outdated information may give the impression that the blog is no longer updated.

CONTACT

The contact page can simply be an email address with other contact details, for example, your skype address and phone number. Alternatively you can use the WordPress contact page plug-in to generate a template form that will link directly to your email inbox. If you do not want to publicly share your email address then this is a good option.

Making yourself available to be contacted is critical, especially for when potential advertisers need to contact you.

ADVERTISE

For those wishing to host advertising on their blog an 'advertise' page can be a useful place to promote advertising options and rates along with a press pack or traffic stats. Useful stats include unique visitors, page views and audience demographics. To track your traffic sign-up for a Google Analytics account. Going one step further you can integrate automatic payment methods with PayPal for immediate booking of advertisement placements.

PRESS

High profile bloggers will be listed in top ten lists, have made appearances on television, the radio and in magazines and newspapers. This is a page where you can link to all the press coverage the blog/business or its owner has received.

Posts

Blogs posts basically refer to the daily or weekly articles that are published to the blog. Posts are written in the dashboard area where you can embed links and add images and multimedia. Posting frequency varies widely from blogger to blogger; however, you need to look at posting around two to three times per week in order to provide fresh content for your readers and the search engines.

That said, even having a blog with one new blog article a week is better than having no blog at all. As social media expert Chris Brogan said earlier in this chapter, blogs have very high authority with search engines, so they are far more effective in attracting search engine traffic than a standard website that is not updated or does not have a blog.

Links

Links are hyperlinked text that lead to another blog or website. You can create a link in most dashboards using the link icon and inserting the web URL you wish to link to. Bloggers will use links whenever they talk about or reference a site or idea from another blog or website. This 'interlinking' within the blogosphere is another reason why blogs rank so well in search engines. Search engine rankings are partially based on the authority each page is seen to have; this authority is gauged by the amount of incoming links the page has and how authoritative the pages are that are linking. This linking creates a 'web' of authority amongst the leading blogs in each niche. This is why it's important to make connections in your niche so that you can become a part of this powerful web and benefit from the linking that occurs.

Images

Images are used to break up text on a blog and to add interest. Bloggers who write about their own lives will often use personal photos or images. You can source images for a small fee from image libraries like istockphoto.com. Alternatively, Creative Commons licensed photos from Flickr may also be used as long as credit is provided. When you source your image from someone else, the copyright is theirs, so it is never correct to simply grab an image from another site: always ask permission first.

RSS

RSS stands for Really Simple Syndication and is a way to help blog readers read several blogs easily in one place. If you want to read blogs via RSS, first you need to sign up for a 'reader'. Google Reader is a popular choice. You then add subscriptions by adding the feed URL to the 'add subscription' box or clicking on the RSS button on the blog you wish to subscribe to. Once subscribed, all the posts from all the blogs you are subscribed to will automatically be delivered to your reader where you can read them in one uninterrupted stream, a bit like a newspaper but one where you get to handpick all the articles!

You should make sure that people can read your site via RSS too. If there is an RSS button built into your own blog then this should be sufficient for people to sign up to read your blog in their reader. If not then you need to 'burn a feed' at the Google Feedburner site. This site can create the code you need to create RSS buttons to add to your blog. Choose whether to offer a 'full feed' or a 'partial feed'. A full feed will mean that your post appears in its entirety inside the reader. A partial feed will appear as a title and a snippet of the post and then the subscriber needs to click through to see the rest. A partial feed is good for increasing page views (and in turn ad revenue); however, most subscribers do not like partial feeds which may hamper your RSS subscriber numbers.

Email updates

Some blogs offer a similar service to RSS that delivers new blog posts to the subscriber's inbox. This is a useful alternative if the blog's audience is less tech savvy. You can get code for an email subscription box from the Google Feedburner site. Simply sign up, burn a feed and go to the 'email subscription' area. You can then copy some code provided and paste this into the sidebar of your blog.

Going live

If you are creating a brand new blog, you can do much of this set-up before setting your blog live. This gives you a chance to experiment and make mistakes without everyone watching. Once you have purchased your domain name, chosen a theme and installed WordPress, completed your pages and written a few posts it is time to go live. You can go live by adjusting the setting in your WordPress or Blogger dashboard.

In time Google will automatically find your blog but to speed up this process you can submit your blog to www.google.co.uk/addurl.

This will alert Google to your blog, your blog posts will start to be indexed in Google and you should start receiving traffic. The traffic you receive from search engines builds up steadily over time so do not expect an avalanche! It will most likely be just one or two visitors a day to start off with.

READING BLOGS

Reading other blogs is seen as an integral part of being a blogger. Not only does it help you become part of the blog community in which you write but it also helps you to hone your own blogging voice. By using a reader this can be easily managed. Simply find a number of blogs in your niche and add them to your Google reader. It is also helpful to subscribe to your own blog not only to get a sense of what the reader receives but also so that you can spot any problems and rectify them.

Blog etiquette

As with all communities there are a number of unspoken rules to which community members adhere. The main rules in the blogging community are:

1. Comment
Receiving and giving comments is a big part of blogging, and many bloggers take the attitude that you have to give to receive. You can usually comment on a blog by clicking a comment link at the top or underneath the post. Each post has its own comments section so comments should be relevant to the post you are commenting on.

2. Give credit
If you reference a site or an idea (even in a small way) then reference should be given to the original site, usually in the form of an embedded link.

3. Do not flame

'Flaming' is when you go around leaving insulting and offensive comments on blogs for the sole purpose of inciting a 'flame war' – a heated and angry exchange between bloggers. This shouldn't be confused with leaving genuine heated comments as part of a debate.

PROMOTING YOUR BLOG

The old adage 'build it and they will come' does not really apply to blogging. A certain amount of traffic will come automatically from search engines but building a loyal audience is somewhat more difficult and takes a bit more effort.

Below are some of the many ways in which bloggers promote and raise the profile of their blogs.

Commenting

Every time you leave a comment on another blog you have the option to link to your blog via your name. Each comment acts as a link back to your blog. Leaving interesting comments will spark interest in readers to find out who you are and what your blog is about. What makes an interesting comment? An interesting comment is one that either extends the discussion somewhat, adds key additional information or advice or one that is anecdotal of personal experience. 'Great post' just does not cut it I am afraid.

Social media channels

Most bloggers are signed up to the main social media channels such as Facebook, Twitter, and if they vlog (publish video posts) then YouTube. Bloggers use these as places to network and socialize as well as promoting links to their latest articles and promoting any products or services they offer.

Blog carnivals

A blog carnival is a roundup of great content in a particular niche. To enter a carnival you simply find out who the host is for that edition and email them your best post on the niche topic. The host then does a carnival post with a short taster and links to all the posts. Not only do you pick up some traffic for that day but you also get a link back and possibly a loyal reader or two. Blog carnivals are a good way to become part of a niche online.

Social bookmarking

Social bookmarking is a way for internet users to save and organize bookmarks to various online resources. An example of a social bookmarking site is Delicious (formerly Del.icio.us). Social bookmarking can be a great way to promote your blog, especially if the social bookmarking site has an element of voting, where users vote in favour of top content. The content with the most votes rises to the top. This is how sites like Digg, Reddit and Kirtsy function.

StumbleUpon is a bookmarking site that works in a slightly different way. Users can surf popular content and the more 'thumbs up' a piece of content gets the more that piece of content is presented to the surfers. This allows some pieces of content to go viral, driving tens and even thousands of surfers to that piece of content.

Twitterfeed

Twitterfeed is a fabulous way of automating the streaming of content from your blog through to Twitter. It is simple to add your feed (usually www.yoururl.com/feed) to Twitterfeed, then every time you post a tweet goes out to all your followers on Twitter, including the title and URL of your post.

Aggregators

Friendfeed helps you manage all the updates from different people you know from different places on the web. It is what is known as a real-time feed aggregator. Nutshellmail is another aggregator. With these services, you get a single email or page that brings together updates from your preferred social media and social networking websites, social bookmarking websites, blogs etc. Aggregators can deal with a range of RSS/Atom feeds.

Competitions

Competitions are a great way to raise the profile and interactivity of your blog. I have hosted many competitions on my blog with much success. A competition creates buzz and excitement and can be a nice departure from your usual content. If you are approached to promote a product you could offer to run a competition instead, if the company are willing to supply the prize. Companies will approach bloggers directly to run competitions on their behalf. Some bloggers will charge for this but if you think the prize is substantial enough then you could do it for free.

The first steps in hosting a competition are securing the prize, deciding who will send out the prize and choosing to whom the competition will be open, i.e. international or national residents only. Then, write the post, including details and links to the prize, ways to enter and a deadline for the competition. You could ask for a blog comment for one entry and a retweet (on Twitter) for a bonus entry. This builds comments on your blog and the retweets help you reach a wider audience. If you are running a competition to help build your mailing list use an online survey form that allows you to gather contact details. Make sure you state in your terms and conditions that you may send mailings to people who have entered competitions. Use a random number generator to pick a winner then contact the winner and sponsor to inform them.

CONTINUING TO BLOG

Blogging is very much a long-term strategy. Traffic is sent to each individual post and incoming links build up over time; therefore, it is something that needs to be built up slowly and steadily, there are no real shortcuts. It takes time to write posts and publish them so building up to the point where you can monetize your blog can take months or even a year or more. But once you have built a loyal following you can add a product range, sell advertising, create a membership site...the list is endless and the earning capacity is practically endless too!

3 Building Your Profile as an Expert and Finding Followers

YOUR EXPERTISE

Becoming an expert on your niche topic is vital if you are to achieve online business success and make money. It can seem difficult, though, to know where to start. If you pick a good niche without too much competition and develop your knowledge and skills regarding how to solve the problems people face, you will find that there is a ready audience of people for your advice. Use your blog as the main place for people to find you and make the most of social media to reach out and develop your followers. Communicate and share your knowledge and tips via your blog, Twitter and, most importantly, by building an email list, and you will find that you are building up the numbers on your mailing list to the point where you can start making a good living online.

What you are aiming to do is develop pre-eminence. As Yaro Starak of www.entrepreneurs-journey.com says,

> Pre-eminence is essentially a perception. It simply means that people believe you are the best or one of the best or at least better than most others, at what you do. It is because of pre-eminence that people choose your business over the competition, that you can charge higher prices and why people seek you out instead of you needing to solicit clients.

How this ties in to your niche

Go back to Chapter 1. Have you got a clear niche that you feel you can monetize? If so, your expert profile has to tie in to this niche. Before you read on further, note down what qualities and knowledge you think people might look for in an expert in this niche. Do some research by looking on forums and social media sites. Who has the most followers in similar niches to this? What are they doing right? By modelling the behaviour of other experts you can learn how to raise your own profile fast. Modelling does not mean becoming a carbon copy: what it does mean is looking at the strategies they use and adapting them for your own needs to come up with your own blueprint for success. Do this in one area, analyse what has worked well for you and you will be able to apply it to new niches too.

Being an expert: just a little bit famous!

So, what does being an expert entail? We are not talking about being a celebrity A-lister but someone who is well known within a specific niche. Helen Lindop explains,

> Instead of being the person whose phone number is on a leaflet on the coffee table, you need to become a little bit famous in that community. You are not going to be mobbed by fans as you walk down the street. But you want yours to be the first name that pops into someone's mind if they have a problem to solve in your specific niche.

Helen adds,

> You could become a bit famous in your niche by getting articles published in the magazines or websites that your niche reads, public speaking at their events, partnering with some-

one else who is already an expert in that niche, starting a blog, arranging events for this community, networking at their events and many more.

Now you might be thinking 'how am I ever going to be a minor celeb in such a clever/talented/good looking group of people?' Yes, this is going to take a little self-confidence. But once you get out there and start talking to people, you find they are *just people*. People like you. And if you have picked your niche well, you will have something valuable to offer that community. You just need to keep listening to them, giving them what they want and giving them great customer service along the way. Take it one step at a time.

Why develop a profile as an expert?

If you are unsure right now why you should develop your profile as an expert, there are plenty of reasons to do so. Most importantly, people trust experts. If you are perceived as an expert people will trust you, and if they trust you they will be one step closer to buying from you. If you have a solution to a 'problem' that they can't get anywhere else, you will find that you start to make sales.

Being seen as an expert can also give you access to far greater exposure than you can get otherwise. As an expert you can offer to help journalists who have queries and get regular media coverage. You will be invited to write articles for other sites, all of which will include your byline, with a little about you and a link back to your website. You may find that you get requests from your local newspaper or radio station if you send them a press release, followed by national media exposure, which can increase the number of hits to your site in a small space of time.

If you are perceived as an expert it will also give a greater monetary value to what you offer. The price someone is willing to pay for your eBook or eCourse will increase if they believe that you are the key person to learn from on this topic. You will be able to create a product funnel where people desire the knowledge you have and as a result will work up from buying your products to becoming willing to pay a premium price for working one to one with you.

How to develop a profile as an expert

In order to be perceived as an expert you need to show that you have knowledge and authority in your area of expertise. There are a number of ways to do this that work well. First, you need to publish material on your topic. Ideally start doing this in a way that anyone can access. A blog full of great content is an ideal start. Offer a free report for people to download with more detailed information when they enter their name and email address.

Once you have started writing blog posts and articles for your own sites and other people's, the next step is to develop some saleable products that also raise your profile. An eBook can be a logical follow-on: by gathering together material you have written already, noting down topics you often get asked about and bringing these together you can quite quickly create an outline for a book. The beauty of eBooks is that, unlike traditional printing, you can determine the length and structure of your publication. The eBook format allows you to avoid printing costs and, if you are smart with your marketing, you can gain almost as much exposure as you would when launching any other sort of book. There are even cost effective ways to get your eBook into print too, and it is not difficult to publish a book that features on Amazon and other popular online book stores. There are many ways to get published nowadays, which we will look at in Chapter 5, because writing a book does an enormous amount to build your authority.

As well as books, you can also build authority through

eCourses. Free eCourses are a great way to build trust with people who join your mailing lists. Paid courses can be the next logical step in your product funnel. Read more about how to structure, create and promote an eCourse in Chapter 4.

When building your profile, it is vital to ensure that you have a good presence online. If there are a number of forums or groups dedicated to your niche, have a good presence in each. Have a good profile on sites such as LinkedIn and Twitter that you update regularly. Be seen as someone who offers good advice, and make sure that you offer this advice without obviously plugging your business. If you have free tip sheets and plenty of articles dealing with issues that people in the niche may face you will have good reasons to point people to your site.

Beyond maximizing your own profile, make sure that other people are backing you up. Endorsements, testimonials and coverage in the press will all change the way people perceive you: 'He's not just blowing his own trumpet, I have seen him on TV' or, 'Someone else I respect really rates him.'

And once you are developing this great expert profile, you need to make sure that you are credible and consistent. If you state that you have certain principles or are perceived as having them, make sure that you stick to them. If you say you will do something, do it and report back to your online audience about how you got on. Sharing your failures as well as your successes will add to your authenticity. Being authentic will build people's trust in you.

Pin down your expertise

Do you now see why being an expert is great for business? It means that people know you as the 'go to' guy or gal for your particular niche. And then you can start drawing them into your product funnel. But you may well be thinking, 'I am not an expert' or 'what could I be an expert in?'

Pinning down your exact area of expertise is a critical stage: choose an area with too much competition and you are making life hard for yourself. Choose an area where you do not have much knowledge and you will spend a long time building your own expertise before you can share with others. This can sometimes work well: if you start a blog about your own journey as a beginner and bring together everything you learn in posts to share with others you can develop a following and a community.

There is lots of competition out there: everyone wants to be an expert on something nowadays, but you can make life easier for yourself if you are clear about your specific area of expertise. Be as focused as possible, and examine the competition. What are their strengths and weaknesses? What makes you different to the next expert?

HOW TO BUILD YOUR PROFILE

Here are more details of the steps you need to take to build your profile.

Blogging

In Chapter 2, we explained all about how to blog. Blogging requires persistence: the most successful bloggers provide fresh content for their readers several times a week, every week. It is easier to stick at blogging if you have great motivation, and the motivation for anyone wanting to make money online *should* be strong. Your blog is the place where you can connect with your readers. By sharing your thoughts, tips and advice you can position yourself as an expert.

Before you start writing, do some research on the keywords you should be using. Go back to Chapter 1 for a quick revision of some keyword research techniques. You should also think about how people will phrase their searches and how this could relate to what you write. If you are writing a self-help blog, for example, do people search more on 'I hate my life' or 'I am feeling depressed' ... or any number of similar terms? Work out which phrases will bring in the focused audience that you need, and remember to include your key phrases in the title or early on in your blog posts. For example, '7 tips to help you if you hate your life', or an article entitled, 'Beating the Black Dog' that starts, 'Do you find yourself saying, "I am feeling depressed" day after day?' both use the key terms that you want to be found for at the top of the page. This makes it easier for people to know that they are on a site that relates to what they are searching for, and it works well for search engines too.

Create regular series of expert tips that keep your readers coming back for more. Jot down ten questions you are always answering, the fifteen most common issues in your niche area or five ways to solve a certain problem. Readers love list posts and you could simply create one post, but why not get your readers coming back for more by making a series of posts, one a week, followed by a round up. This could even then feed into an eBook or eCourse: all building your authority.

Beyond the technical side of creating your blog, you also need to write with passion. As Dale Carnegie said, 'When dealing with people, let us remember we are not dealing with creatures of logic. We are dealing with creatures of emotion, creatures bustling with prejudices and motivated by pride and vanity.' Write about your own emotions if you are creating the sort of blog that details your own learning journey or how you are working through a particular problem. One of the key differentiators between a blog and other online magazine sites is the personal element: a blog is where you can really let your 'self' shine through. It is this that will encourage people to subscribe to your feed or newsletter: they like you and what you write.

To do this, you may well need to look carefully at your own

comfort levels about sharing. Exposing elements of yourself online builds trust: look at influential blogger Yaro Starak of www.entrepreneurs-journey.com who posts regular updates on his online earnings. As someone who is offering courses to help you earn online, it is important that he offers proof that he 'walks the talk' and is growing his own earnings using the techniques he is teaching. How would this apply to your area of expertise? What proof could you offer your readers that you practise what you teach?

You do need to consider what you write when building an expert profile, though. There are a number of successful blogs that are built on rants or gossip, but this sort of site won't work for everyone and can actually deter some people from following you. Do feel confident about writing about your successes, including media coverage, or mentioning when you are speaking at an event. Think carefully, and even get someone else's opinion before writing about personally painful experiences. Sharing your bad times does build trust but you can regret these things later. If in doubt, leave a post as a draft and come back to it a day or two later if it contains strong emotions. One further point: do check out the libel laws in the country you are writing in and the country of anyone mentioned in the article. When publishing posts on your blog, you need to be clear that everything you write is based on fact and that you can back up what you write.

Use your blog as a way of interacting with your readers. You can highlight a dilemma and get reader solutions, suggest some solutions and ask for more, or ask for further topics that you should cover. Each time someone makes a comment, make sure that you respond, thus building the relationship with your readers and developing your profile not only as someone who gives expert advice, but as someone who listens and responds to readers. If you ask for article suggestions, make sure that you highlight that when you write the post, and perhaps mention the person who asked for it. In the same vein, go out and share positive and helpful advice on other people's blogs. If relevant, you can then lead them back to an article on your own site, or even write a new article in response. All this will help develop your expert profile.

Guest articles for other blogs, newsletters and business websites

As well as creating your own blog, another way to build your expert profile and draw in new followers is to offer guest posts and articles for other blogs, newsletters and websites. There are many sites such as ezinearticles.com where you can place articles, creating links back to your own site and allowing others the opportunity to use your article. This is fine for raising the number of links into your site, but it is not what I am focusing on here.

Instead of using general article websites to generate links, get smart. Build up your own list of blogs and websites that your target audience might visit. Start to develop a relationship with the site owner: maybe pop over every week and leave helpful comments on his or her site for a few weeks before getting in touch and offering to write an article or guest post on your niche topic. If, for example, your site focuses on ways to distress your model railway engines to make them appear weathered, collect a list of relevant sites and blogs for model railway enthusiasts. Build links, offer a unique article and, when it is published on the site, make sure you link to it from your own site. You will be showing your readers that other opinion formers in the field rate your specialist knowledge. Even more important, you will be drawing in readers from the new site who may then become regulars on your blog. Make this as effective as possible by using the byline and site link at the bottom of the article to draw people across. Under the article about weathering engines, you could write, 'This article is by Fred Smith, author of *17 Routes to Effective Weathering*. Claim your free eBook to help you weather your own engines from Fred's site, www.weatheredengine.com.' You will find well-targeted readers who will sign up for your free product, and be drawn in to your product funnel.

Check which sites in related niches take guest posts and which could be looking for articles for their newsletter. Remember, these site owners are valuable contacts: respect them by offering unique articles as far as possible – no one likes to find they are running a feature that can also be found on another site. In the future you may also want to invite them to join your affiliate programme (see Chapter 8).

Social proof and testimonials

According to Wikipedia, 'Social proof, also known as informational social influence, is a psychological phenomenon that occurs in ambiguous social situations when people are unable to determine the appropriate mode of behaviour. Making the assumption that surrounding people possess more knowledge about the situation, they will deem the behaviour of others as appropriate or better informed.' Simply put, if we are unsure, we look at what other people are doing and use that to guide our own behaviour and decisions.

How does this affect you and your blog? What it means is that, every so often, you need to include comments from others, statistics about your sales and positive reviews. If, for example, you run a blog and sell a membership course, run video and written reviews from members. If you have products, offer people the chance to add their reviews under each product: do like Amazon does and get in touch with people a little while after they purchase and invite them back to the product page to submit a review. If you use a shopping cart like 1ShoppingCart with an autoresponder you can set this up to happen automatically.

Why bother getting reviews? Well, people visiting your site will tend to develop more trust if they can get independent opinions from people who have bought from you and tried the products out. It is that simple.

What is more, if you are selling a product or course you can highlight just how many people have bought or joined already. When we launched our Become a Mumpreneur course we posted about the number of sign-ups on the sales page and updated it every couple of days during the initial launch period. Showing that a hundred people had joined in just a few days helped waverers to commit, knowing they would be part of a group who had all decided that subscribing was the right choice.

How does this build your profile as an expert? It is simple. You are no longer just saying 'I am an expert', but you have followers who are also saying the same thing. An independent view or review will make people trust what you are saying. Use reviews alongside your free giveaway item in your sidebar. Feature them as regular posts on your blog. Add relevant testimonials under each product you have for sale. Continually reinforce the message that it is not just *you* saying that you are an expert until other people believe it too and are willing to stand up and tell the world!

More about user reviews

Whenever you create a new product or programme, get people to test it out on a small scale before you launch. There are lots of benefits to this. Your followers will feel that they are being given an exclusive opportunity if you invite them to share their views when developing a product *and* show that you have listened to them when you create the final version. Then you will be able to use some of the user reviews as part of your product launch. From the first moment you share news about the product, you will be able to say, 'Do not just take my word for it. Jim tried it out and he says ...'. It is vital to always get permission from people before using their reviews in your promotion. Ask for permission *and* a photograph. Offer incentives for people who review your offerings such as a bonus or free use of a product. Invite video testimonials – these can be much more powerful than the written word for many audiences.

Expert reviews, endorsements and testimonials

Moving beyond reviews from your buyers, users and followers, it is also really helpful to get reviews from people who are influential in your field. If a review from an ordinary Joe helps build your credibility, think how much more you will gain if your review is from someone known in your field. Build up a shortlist of people you respect and who have a good following. Do not be deterred by thoughts like 'He'll never get back to me'. If you do not ask, you will never find out. Get in touch with the person – via email if you can, via an agent if necessary, and ask if they'll review your book or course or other product. Make it as easy as possible for them by supplying what they need, when they need it. If you are writing a longer book, you may just want them to review the first few chapters while you complete the book. That way you will be able to use their reviews on the cover and in PR. Most importantly, of course, add each review and an image of the person to your website. Be clear that this is what you want to do when you first approach someone as you always need permission to use someone's name and image. A video testimonial is even better.

HOW TO BUILD YOUR FOLLOWERS

Twitter, blogs and Facebook are all examples of social media, also known as 'web 2.0', where content can be created by anyone who takes part in each community. These sites are key tools that will help you reach many more people and spread your business message. Read on for an insight into why they work, and how to use them effectively to build your reputation.

How many followers do you think you need to make a living online? Different people may have different estimates, and it can depend on what you are offering. In one theory, Kevin Kelly of www.kk.org suggests that an artist, musician or designer etc.

might need 1,000 true fans to be successful. That is 1,000 people who buy your work, employ your services, read your blog, and retweet your tweets. Brian Austin Whitney of www.jpfolks.org suggests that the critical number is 5,000. Whatever the figure, if you can build up a group of people who love what you do and invest in everything you bring out, you have a solid basis for an online business. We believe this approach applies to people selling information just as much as those selling art or music. Kelly calculates that if these 1,000 true fans spent one day's wage per year on your products or services then that roughly equates to: £100 x 1,000 true fans = £100,000 per year. Not only that but once you reach this kind of number you will experience a 'tipping point', a point where you find that your fans begin to spread your marketing messages for you, allowing you to take a step back to focus on your product or service.

Social media can help you build your fan army; beyond that, the people you 'recruit' from Facebook and Twitter and other social media sites are web savvy and used to sharing information and recommending companies. This is not the only way to recruit fans – speaking engagements, live events and print and broadcast media coverage all help you develop an expert profile and attract followers. The beauty of social media, though, is that you communicate with people on a regular basis, create relationships with your fans and draw them in to your website. So, when speaking at an event, for example, end with a call to people to follow you on Facebook or Twitter.

It is really important to make the most of social media for your business. You wouldn't turn down someone offering you a handful of tenners, would you? Nor would you walk on by if someone came up to you in the street and said, 'I have heard about what you offer and it sounds right up my street – can you tell me more?' If you are not blogging and tweeting, you are actually turning away potential sales and missing the chance to tell customers all about your product and why it is just what they need.

Twitter

Twitter is a leading social media site with 190 million member accounts. It is especially popular with bloggers and businesses. It can be difficult to describe: you write short updates about what you are doing, so it is sometimes called 'microblogging'. If you write your updates via www.twitter.com the 140 character limit for tweets makes it feel like texting – although there are now more sites allowing you to create longer tweets too. You can drop in and out of Twitter, have it on in the background, or programme in scheduled tweets in advance. The best way to find out what Twitter means to you is to jump in and try it.

Use a mix of tweets to build followers. Combine personal tweets for authenticity with questions inviting others to interact with you. Asking questions can help you refine your offering – that's market research. It also makes people feel that they can ask you questions, giving you a chance to offer advice and tips. Make sure that you link to 'good stuff' from other people: depending on your audience this could be a funny video, a beautiful photo or an incisive article. Promote what other people are doing to add value to what you offer your followers. Retweeting other people's messages also makes it easier to ask for similar favours in return. Finally, of course, combine all these types of tweets with messages promoting the great content you offer on your blog to build your expert profile, and those highlighting current and forthcoming projects – these are the ones that will make you money.

Key points for raising your profile as an expert on Twitter:

- Upload a photo to your account. Use a clear headshot. Without a photo people will assume you are a spammer, someone who sends unasked-for promotional messages

- Write a tweet introducing yourself and saying that you are new to Twitter, engage in conversation with anyone who responds and take it from there

- Link Twitter to your blog so your new posts get tweeted automatically
- Build in tweets to older articles too
- Find other people who tweet on similar topics and follow them
- Try out Tweetdeck, Hootsuite and SocialOomph, which offer a range of ways to use Twitter more effectively
- And of course you can follow us @erica and @antoniachitty

Facebook

Facebook is a great way of reaching out to people. An increasing proportion of the population use the site – over 600 million people at the time of writing – and you can find people looking for consumer products and services. It costs you nothing to set up a Facebook page and it can bring in new visitors to your main website and build a base of loyal customers.

It is straightforward to set up a Facebook page for your products or services by following the step by step guidance. Start from www.facebook.com/pages/create.php. You can use the site to post questions asking contacts for views on your business ideas: one member of a course we run did this and got seven orders straight away! Each time you add a message to your page or profile this may appear in the stream of information on your friends' and followers' homepages. When they comment or 'like' what you have written their friends can see the link too, allowing your messages to spread virally.

If you have a personal Facebook account and have just set up a business page, invite friends who you know might be interested in the topic to follow you. Ask them to invite their relevant friends, share links to your new groups via other social media, and offer a prize draw when you reach your first 100 or 500 followers.

Use a service like Networked Blogs to link your blog to your

Facebook page so people can see your fresh content via Facebook if they prefer: this means that your updates can go to them where they are, rather than expecting them to visit your site every time. If people are interested in the short extracts from your blog on Facebook they can click and go through to your blog for the full article.

Get smart and include options to sign up for your newsletter or free eBooks and eCourses on your Facebook page too: give people every opportunity to slide into the top end of your product funnel.

Ecademy

Ecademy is a great place to develop an expert profile, particularly if you offer a business-to-business product or service. It is well set up for you to highlight your expertise with its 'Know Me, Like Me, Follow Me' mantra. The site has fully embraced social media, and in a lot of ways was a forerunner in creating a site with user generated content.

If you are unfamiliar with Ecademy, the site describes itself as, 'a membership organization for entrepreneurs and business owners who belong to a community that connects, supports and transacts with one another'. The site was founded in 1998 by Thomas and Penny Power as the Institute of Ecommerce. It aims to help users make new contacts, find work, advertise their services, get business support and advice and meet at live events.

Ideal for reaching business people, you can take out a free membership to Ecademy, but many of the services are only available to paid subscribers. If you know that you need to market to entrepreneurs and business owners, do consider trying it out for six months or a year. You can join groups relevant to your niche, get introduced to 'friends of friends', post adverts in the marketplace and more. The live events are run by Ecademy members for Ecademy members: you can even run your own social business networking events via the site.

LinkedIn

LinkedIn is another community of business people. It is somewhere that employees, business owners and employers can create a personal profile and indicate that they are interested in:

- business deals
- career opportunities
- consulting offers
- expertise requests
- getting back in touch
- new ventures
- job enquiries
- reference requests

The site has been up and running since 2003 and, in January 2011, reported more than 90 million registered users, spanning more than 200 countries and territories worldwide.

Join LinkedIn if you want to reach professionals and working people. You can use the site to contact 'friends of friends', as with Ecademy. For anyone wanting to build an expert profile online it is important to be present on significant sites like LinkedIn. A complete profile with your photograph, your history and client or customer recommendations helps people trust you. Get involved in relevant groups and share good tips and advice. Go to the answers section and proactively help people with questions. Showcase your expertise, and link to articles on your blog if you have written something relevant to the question asked.

Ecademy, LinkedIn or both?

On one level, you may think Ecademy and LinkedIn have significant areas of overlap and wonder which one you should use. My advice is to try both. The sites have a different 'feel', which is hard to describe, and both can help you find a great group of contacts and grow your business. Use sites like Ecademy and LinkedIn to follow your competitors too. There is plenty of scope in online business to be a follower of a competitor and recommend their products where they fill a gap that you haven't covered. You will build up favours, be seen as a positive person to link with, and can even earn through affiliate sales.

More useful sites for networking, building your profile and staying in touch

- *Plaxo:* an online address book and social networking service. Can help you keep up to date with followers' contact details

- *MySpace:* online networking site with over 100 million members, a favourite for musicians and pop groups. Do the people you want to find fit this site?

- *YouTube:* Video is a great medium for anyone wanting to make money online, and YouTube is a good place to start hosting your videos, sharing them and interacting. You can add keywords to your videos so people can find them when they search, which can help you build followers too

- *Bebo:* a social network with a younger age profile than business sites and an estimated 117 million members

There are plenty more social networks: look on Wikipedia for a current list with estimates of active user accounts and the market that each network serves. Make a shortlist of sites and explore them. If you create a profile, do make sure you keep it up to date: an old profile can detract from the trust that you are working hard to create. Do not try to be present on all the sites at once: do try different ones out and see where you can make connections naturally and find the sort of person who is a relevant and useful follower.

DEVELOPING YOUR EXPERT PROFILE FURTHER

Alongside developing your online profile, you also need to make the most of other opportunities to be perceived as an expert. Do not dismiss traditional promotion tools such as press releases, print advertising and flyers. Attend, speak at and organize events. You will find these tools and this sort of exposure invaluable in bringing people on to your website and into your sales funnel. Read *A Guide to Promoting Your Business* and *PR and Marketing: The Essential Guide* to learn more practical ways to promote yourself. Study other experts and see what you can learn from people you admire. Do one thing to raise your online expert profile each day and you will build followers and develop pre-eminence.

Case Study: Nigel Botterill

www.nigelbotterill.com

Nigel Botterill is a serial entrepreneur. In this interview he explains how the internet has played a key role in his success.

Nigel started his career at Barclays, worked with John Caudwell as the Marketing Director for Singlepoint, part of his Phones4U empire, and then worked with self-made multi-millionaire Hamish Ogston at Card Protection Plan, which inspired him to break out and set up his own marketing consultancy business, N5 Ltd, in 2003. Since then he has set up six different businesses including My Mag, thebestof and Raring2go! magazine.

Nigel is always open to new business ideas and is keen to trial ideas that he and his team come up with. If you are assessing a business idea, Nigel has some advice,

A good business idea is something that people want to buy. Huge demand is best. We at N5 have lots of ideas. We will get the idea ready and launched: my maxim is 'good is good enough'. I go for the 'ready, fire, aim' strategy. You just need to get it out there. Only when you try something will you find if it has legs. Some of my ideas have been way more successful than I anticipated but there is no such thing as a sure thing. One of the mistakes businesspeople can make is to spend way too long preparing to get something out there. It is a waste of time and energy and money. If you have an idea, create a one page website and test it out.

While many of Nigel's businesses have a strong online component, he advises, 'There is no such thing as an online business. It is very hard to just transact online. The internet forms a huge part of our sales funnel but we use offline press ads to draw people into our websites where we encourage them to share their contact details, and we will follow them up personally, offline.'

Nigel's first business was a marketing consultancy. He explains how this led to the next business, one which was scalable:

When I set up N5 it was simply a vehicle for me to consult. As I left employment my wife Sue was starting her own local magazine. She was asked to advise one or two other people on how to set up a My Mag magazine like hers. I didn't have great expectations for this: perhaps we could sell half a dozen My Mag set ups each year. We placed an ad in a parenting magazine. A few people came to see us and we sold two kits. I spent the next few days finishing the pack, and invested their fees back in advertising. We sold more, and I reinvested in more advertising and created our first website which led to loads and loads of enquiries. The income from My Mag quickly became bigger than my consulting income so I decided to focus full time on My Mag. I sacked all my clients by handing them on to someone else.

We parted on good terms and I knew I could build up a consultancy again, but within 3 weeks I was working on My Mag full time.

The magazines worked well so we decided to take it online to become thebestof.co.uk. A buyer is a buyer so the first people I approached to buy into thebestof were My Mag operators. 47 bought thebestof and this gave us the momentum to grow. We now have 300 franchise areas. Thebestof was initially an online directory, one of the first in the marketplace but within 6 months there were lots of other players. We relaunched in 2007 so it now offers a full marketing suite for local businesses.

What makes for a successful thebestof franchisee? Nigel has found three important qualities:

They are entrepreneurial. We give them a tool kit but nothing in there replaces the ability to spot an opportunity on the ground and exploit it. They are likeable. It is a lot about the businessperson involved. Businesses have to like and buy into the person running thebestof. They are hard working. Especially in the current climate you can't build a successful business without hard work. There is a lot of truth in Tim Ferriss's book *The 4 Hour Workweek*, but the title always gets the headline. I know that you do have to work hard to build a business.

Nigel's most recent enterprise is The Entrepreneurs Circle, which arose out of a mistake that demonstrated a market need:

Christmas 2008 when the media was at its gloomiest we wanted to do something to help franchisees. We invited them all to a training day which was really positive and motivating for the people who attended. At the end of the day one of the team took videos of people as they left, talking about the day. We planned to send the video out to franchisees who hadn't come to the day and invite them to another event, but by mistake the video got sent to all the businesses who do business with thebestof franchisees. The team sent out an apology within half an hour, but over that weekend we had 11000 hits on the video, and there were 1000 responses. Out of those, three or four dozen were asking whether they could come to a training day. In the end we held 4 events with around 150 attendees at each, followed by another 10 events in the summer of 2009 under the title 'Screw Surviving'.

I realised that there is a huge market of business owners, bereft of guidance and direction. Success is not just about being good at what you do, it is also about marketing and promotion. We now have around 1000 members of the entrepreneurs circle and plans for 10,000. The Internet plays a useful role in this. We find customers through the internet; we use it to share resources. It is a great way of delivering content through webinars which allows us to offer much greater value to members. For each webinar we can send people workbooks too.

If you are inspired by Nigel's story, he has two key pieces of advice,

My second most important bit of advice is that you have to set yourself tight challenging deadlines. Deadlines are how you get things done. Most importantly, though, when I started my own business I had a deep sense of inadequacy. Employment was a poor preparation for running a business. I set out to learn from people who had been there before me. Most business owners do not do any learning at all. Find and follow proven success strategies. This can bring your reality closer to your aspirations.

4 Creating an eCourse

WHAT IS AN ECOURSE?

An eCourse is a course that can be delivered completely online via email. In its simplest form it may just be a series of emails on a particular topic. A more complex eCourse may include multimedia materials like videos, podcasts and perhaps even a forum and/or members area.

WHY CREATE AN ECOURSE?

An eCourse allows you to break down complex topics and entire subject areas into easily digestible chunks. Humans learn in different ways and for some a book is a great way to learn a new skill or consume knowledge on a topic. Others find books overwhelming. An eCourse allows knowledge to be delivered and consumed in bite-size chunks. With the addition of multimedia and a members' area it can be a truly dynamic way to learn.

From a creator's point of view eCourses can be very enjoyable to develop, especially if you are passionate about a topic or love to teach. Creating and selling an eCourse is one way to turn a hobby or passion into a flexible way of earning an income online. Here's how psychologist Jean O'Brien has turned her knowledge into an income stream using the eCourse format:

I have written educational courses for several years and sold them on to Distance Learning companies. As a Psychologist, Psychotherapist and mediator as well as a qualified lecturer I wanted to share my knowledge with students and felt this was an excellent way to do this. After contacting several companies I was fortunate enough to receive my first commission, writing a 30,000 word course in Child Psychology for a Royalty of 5%. This required a huge leap of faith on my part. If I wrote the course which would take me about 6 weeks and if it didn't sell, I would receive nothing!

Taking a brave step I settled down to writing and found I really loved it! Before long I was writing for many of the biggest companies both in the UK and abroad. People were actually ringing me for work! Some of the courses were bought outright and some were commission only. As I also worked as a Psychotherapist and Counsellor I kept my writing to about 3 days a week, reserving 3 days to work in my private clinics in London and Sussex. I loved my face to face work and had some high profile clients in the music and television business, so had the best of both worlds.

Two years ago my youngest daughter became seriously ill which meant I had to close my practices to look after her. Writing then became my only source of income. Unfortunately this happened about the same time as the recession so work became scarce and some Distance Learning companies even closed. I began thinking there must be other mums like me, who would like to work around their family commitments, so began writing courses that could be developed into businesses. As time permitted the business could grow. I started writing courses for myself and selling them directly to students via my website www.fromadistance.org. This has worked out wonderfully well as not only do I write the courses but tutor them too. I have a much closer relationship with my students as I know them from beginning to end. The courses I write include Child Psychology, Counselling, Life Coaching, Mediation, Wellbeing and Hypnobirth. Although my daughter is still poorly I have begun to see a few of my clients again as I think it is essential to keep your skills up to date.

HOW TO CREATE AN ECOURSE

You may already have a hobby, passion or area of expertise that may make for a great eCourse. If not, then it is time to start thinking about what topic area might make for a great online course.

Factors to consider

Do people want it?

You may think you have the best idea in the world for an eCourse but what you really need to find out is if people want it. There is no point in creating an eCourse only to find that there is no demand for it. Creating an online course takes quite a bit of time. You have to come up with the idea, create a plan, write the content and develop the whole process from sign-up through to delivery of the course. So it is worth being sure about your topic before you begin. A popular niche does not always make a popular eCourse. Some topic areas lend themselves to eCourses, some less so. It really helps the likelihood of success if there is some 'pain' involved in the topic area. For example, is it something that is very difficult or complex to understand? Are there 'insider' or 'expert' secrets to be shared? Your course needs a 'hook', something that urges someone to buy your product.

You can establish the potential demand for an eCourse by doing some market research:

- Is there a thriving community interested in the niche area you are considering? Consider how many people you would need to buy your product to make it profitable
- Use the Google Keyword Tool to check for search traffic in your niche area
- Are there many people searching for information on this particular topic?

- Are there any books or forums on the niche topic you are considering?

- Do people spend money on products and services in this niche? Does the target market have disposable income to spend on your product?

Is it an under-serviced market?

Once you have established whether there is a market or not, you need to establish how well serviced that market is. For example, does the market have access to all the information they require in all formats, including podcasts, videos, eBooks and eCourses? People learn in different ways, make sure all bases are covered. A book on Amazon is not evidence that the market has all the resources they require. Find out:

- Are there eBooks on the topic?

- Are there books on Amazon on the topic?

- Are there any well established forums?

- Has anyone else created an eCourse already? If they have, how good is it? Does it include multimedia, a membership site and a forum? Can you immediately see ways that you can improve upon their offering?

- Are there resources available to suit all types of learner; audio, visual, kinaesthetic?

Will people pay for it?

You have established that there is a market and that the market is under serviced (or you have gone back to the drawing board to find a new niche topic). Now you need to find out whether people will pay for your offering, and this is a tricky one. The obvious answer is to try and survey your target market. One way to do this is approach the owner of an established forum and ask if you can survey their members. This has the obvious pitfall of the owner of the forum recognizing the opportunity and potentially creating their own eCourse, but do not panic: most people are not in the position where they will create an eCourse just because somebody has asked a question about one.

Another way is to create a 'market research blog'. You basically have a survey on a blog or website and drive traffic there either via a 'pay per click' traffic campaign via Google adwords or by trying to access email lists of your target market that you could ask to complete the survey. A longer term strategy is to create a blog and build traffic organically, but this in itself can take six months or more. If you have an idea for a future project then start your market research blog nice and early so that you can get as much free traffic as you can.

HOW MUCH WILL PEOPLE PAY FOR IT?

Whilst you are surveying people to find out whether they would pay for your eCourse you also need to find out *how much* they would be willing to pay. To get an accurate indicator you will need to have a clear idea of what would be included and communicate that to those taking the survey. It may be that you have a number of options and you just ask people to manually write in a price. If you give people price points to choose from they are more likely to choose the lowest, whereas if you ask them to put a value on the offering then you will have a much more accurate (and probably higher) figure on what people really believe your product is worth.

HOW LARGE IS THE TARGET MARKET AND WHAT PERCENTAGE WILL BUY?

Next you need to establish the size of your target market. You can do this by doing some secondary research into the quantitative data already available such as reports and statistical data.

You can do your own primary research too. Check levels of search traffic, the size of forums etc.

You now need to work out a 'conversion rate' (what percentage of people when offered your product will buy it). To work this out *before* your product is on the market is difficult, and to get an exact conversion rate is impossible. A market research blog helps from the point of view that, if you make the visitors to that site an offer such as 'sign up for this free eBook on X' or 'Register your interest for Y eCourse', the sign-up rate is an indicator of what your eventual conversion rate could be.

It is easy to fool yourself into excessive optimism just to see an idea come to fruition, but make this mistake and you are only hampering your own chance of success. Creating an eCourse takes time and to give yourself the best chance of succeeding you need to try and pick a strong niche from the outset.

HOW WILL PEOPLE PAY FOR IT?

Once you have a rough conversion rate it is time to think about how and what you will charge. On the 'how' you have the choice of an upfront fee, for example £99 for the whole course, or a monthly subscription, such as £9.99. There are pros and cons to both. The upfront fee ensures that people stay the course but it can make for a very unstable income for you with many peaks and troughs. A monthly subscription is a lower psychological barrier to entry for the customer (their initial investment is much smaller). However, they can cancel their payment at any time so you need to consider cancellations in your costing and income forecasts.

How long will the course be?

If you decide to opt for the monthly subscription then you will need to consider how long your eCourse will be as this will determine how many (maximum) subscriptions each customer will pay, and therefore how much you can earn. Remember that not all members will stay the course, so just because your eCourse is ten months long that does not equate to ten monthly subscriptions of £X.

CREATING YOUR ECOURSE

If you have done your market research and you are confident that you have a viable product then it is time to start creating your eCourse. At the same time you should be focusing on building an email list – these are the people to whom you will sell your eCourse. You can do this via a blog plus email newsletter or you can joint venture with someone who already has an email list populated with your target market. Refer to Chapter 3 on how to build your profile as an expert and how to find followers. This step is crucial to the success of your eCourse.

Case Study, Yaro Starak of Entrepreneur's Journey

www.entrepreneurs-journey.com

Internet entrepreneur Yaro Starak started his blog in January 2004. It was created to chronicle his journey through the business world. Before blogging, he ran a hobby focused website and then launched his first business, Better Edit, a company providing editing services to foreign students. He was surprised, though, to find that Better Edit wasn't going to be his main moneymaker. He explains, 'My blog grew faster than I could have imagined and it wasn't long before the blog was earning more than the business.' Just eight months after the launch Yaro started making his first few dollars from Entrepreneur's Journey. At this point Yaro had around 300 visitors a day and about 1,000 RSS subscribers and he was earning around $1,000 a month. His income began with selling banner advertising before he progressed on to affiliate marketing and then creating his own products.

Yaro spotted the opportunity to create the first ever eCourse on blogging. He says, 'The report I wrote as part of the launch went viral in my niche, building my email list significantly, I still get up to 100 new subscribers a day to my list which gives me peace of mind as I know that I have a constant stream of new people to sell to'. Blog Mastermind was developed during 2006/07 and the first members were invited to join in Summer 2007. The first launch attracted over 400 members. Although Yaro lost around 30% of these members in the first few months he says, 'I was able to successfully pinpoint what was causing the attrition and plug the gaps. One of the issues was that the course was open ended. Psychologically this was a barrier for members to overcome so I adjusted this shortly after the launch to make it a fixed term course and attrition dropped significantly.' Yaro estimates that the entire course including the launch took approximately 200 hours to create and market, and grossed over $250,000 over its four-year lifetime.

Yaro went on to launch Membership Site Mastermind, an eCourse based around his experiences of creating Blog Mastermind, teaching others how to create similar subscription based programmes in their own niche. Following this, Become a Blogger was created with a business partner, Gideon Shalwick. Yaro cites this course as being his most successful in terms of numbers, demonstrating the value in joint venture partnerships. Over seven years Yaro has built his income up to approx $20,000 a month. He says, 'I currently spend around two hours a day on the business. I have even managed to travel around the world and manage the business on the road.'

Establishing a structure for your eCourse

Your first task is to map out what your eCourse will look like. You need to consider the following:

- How much information you will include: how 'deep' will you go?

- How this information breaks down into sub-topic areas or 'modules'

- Which order the modules or sub-topics will be delivered in. The order of delivery must bear in mind the needs of the subscriber; they cannot run if they haven't learned to stand up yet

- How will you break the content down sufficiently? Many subscribers will find that tackling one aspect of the topic, or one task, per email is enough

- Mind mapping can be a useful tool for working out which topics you want to cover and the best order in which to deliver them. If you are not familiar with mind mapping then a more basic strategy is to write the topic areas down on post-it notes that you can arrange and re-arrange until they form a course outline that you are happy with.

Writing your eCourse

Once you have the structure in place writing your eCourse should be relatively simple. Tackle each sub-topic in turn. Assume your readers have no prior knowledge otherwise your content can become complex and jargony. This is definitely something you want to avoid. Writing your eCourse in order also helps you to maintain a good 'flow', especially if you can imagine yourself as the student taking the course as you write it. If you do this you will often remember additional bits of information that you can easily slot into new eLessons.

Most eCourse creators won't write a complete eCourse before selling it. The reason for this is that they do not want to invest a lot of time upfront into a product that does not sell. So they create enough content to get started with and will ensure that it sells well before creating the rest. Secondly, until they have paying customers it is difficult to gauge *exactly* what they require. By completing just six weeks of content you can adjust and tailor the content as you go along. This makes for a better eCourse that is more suited to the target market.

Learning methods

People learn in different ways and it will help both the sales of and customer satisfaction with your course if you can cover all learning styles within your eCourse.

Visual: Visual learners learn by seeing. This can be reading text from a page or watching a video. Examples of visual content:

- eBooks
- eLessons
- downloadable PDFs
- videos
- images
- slideshows
- PowerPoint presentations

Auditory: Some people learn best by listening. Examples of auditory content:

- podcasts
- teleclasses

Kinaesthetic: Some people learn best when they work and interact with others. Examples of content that encourages interaction:

- group activities
- forums
- blogs

Bringing together all three learning styles, for example in the form of a webinar (a live internet presentation with PowerPoint or other screen stimulus), can be an effective way of covering all learning styles and being inclusive. A live webinar will allow participants to 'hear' the teacher, 'watch' the screen and 'interact' by asking questions/participating in a discussion after the webinar. These webinars can also be recorded to create timeless content that you can share again and again.

Tools

Technically, delivering an eCourse is not too difficult. Here's what you will need:

AN EMAIL SERVICE PROVIDER

This is how the eLessons are delivered automatically. Once a member has subscribed to your course they automatically move through the email sequence. This is how an eCourse can bring in a good passive income: once created, the upkeep is minimal. To create your sequence you simply paste each of your eLessons into a new 'followup'. You can decide how many days' interval you want between lessons, so if it is a weekly course you just insert a '7' and the next eLesson will automatically be delivered seven days after the previous one. Subscribers can join your eCourse by completing a sign-up form, which is provided by your ESP.

An ESP also allows you to have subscribers at all different stages of the course so you can either choose to have periods where you open your eCourse to new members or you can have it open all the time. There are pros and cons to both approaches. Having short periods where your course is open creates the feeling of scarcity and can urge people to make a decision when perhaps they would have otherwise stalled. However, having your course closed for long periods of time could result in the loss of some customers who do not want to wait for you to re-open and so will find an alternative. There is no universal right or wrong answer. Your best bet is to test both strategies and see which works best in your niche.

There are many email service providers such as Aweber, Constant Contact and Mailchimp. There is more on choosing and using ESPs in Chapter 11.

A PAYMENT PROVIDER

If you are selling your eCourse then you will need a way of taking payments. This can be a simple PayPal button or a more complex system using 1ShoppingCart or Clickbank. You may want to look into getting a business bank account and a merchant account. Your choice will depend on whether you want to recruit affiliates to promote your products and what other functionality you require. There is more on this topic in Chapter 11.

TOOLS TO CREATE MULTIMEDIA

If you want to offer videos then you will need a digital camera; a handheld Flip is a good, simple-to-use option that requires minimal investment; the cameras on up-to-date phones can also get you started. If you want to do video tutorials, for example, clips of you showing your members how to do things on your screen, then you will need additional software like Jing or Camtasia. Camtasia offers you a number of editing options such as the ability to add text, highlight your cursor and add sound effects that are good for practical eCourses. You can also edit your videos to switch from your desktop to you speaking to a PowerPoint presentation and back again. Camtasia really allows you to flex your teaching muscles and provide exciting and engaging content for your course students.

Once you have created your videos you will need somewhere to host them. Sites like YouTube and Vimeo offer a free hosting platform but bear in mind that anyone will be able to view your videos and this could devalue your eCourse. Hosting your videos on a public platform could also raise questions over the professionalism of your course. Private hosting options include Viddler, Cachefly and Vzaar. You can pay for these services monthly or annually and they provide a secure way for you to host your videos whilst ensuring only paying members can view them.

WEBINARS

If you want to go the extra mile and offer your members live webinars then you will need a subscription to a site like GoToWebinar. For a monthly fee you can host as many live webinars as you want. Webinars are a great way to bring in experts in particular areas of your niche and interview them. Most webinar software allows listeners to ask and answer questions and raise their hands. Done well an online webinar is a great, low-cost alternative (for both you and your members) to the traditional seminar. If you record your webinars and package them up this gives you yet another product to sell. This is another example of a passive income, as once recorded and packaged you can make webinar sales ongoing for no extra work.

MEMBERSHIP SITES

A membership site is an excellent way to really raise the value of your course. You can host a membership site from a password protected WordPress blog where you can install forum software. Alternatively you can use a platform like Ning, or professional membership software like WishList Member. A membership site really taps into a lot of psychological triggers such as the need to belong and share the learning process. It also covers the interactive style of learning that we mentioned earlier. Whether it is a simple email-based eCourse or a more complex membership site model, an eCourse is a fairly simple and enjoyable product to create. Choose a good topic and it can become a labour of love.

Case Study: Amelia Critchlow, who turned her love of art into an eCourse

www.ameliacritchlow.co.uk

When asked how she got started Amelia said 'Last year I had a moment where I realised that working for others, coming home to my own children, *and* running a home was really taking its toll on me'. Facing this most common of situations Amelia decided to take her art training and try and turn it into an eCourse that would provide her an income for doing something she loved that would also work round her family. Amelia, 'worked hard, saved some money, got back up childcare' and once the support was in place she set about creating the content for the course. As a trained tutor with experience running live art workshops Amelia had a solid base of experience that she could transfer into the eCourse format.

A year before she planned to run her first eCourse she started blogging and building her audience. Then at the end of the year and once most of the content was written Amelia 'put the feelers out and put out a registration form for those inter-ested'. Once there were enough people interested she released the dates for the first course. Amelia has automated the course as much as possible, 'There is a PayPal button so enrolment/getting a place on the course is really simple for the buyer, and this means payment occurs up front and is easy and can be accessed by anyone in the world who is online and has a PayPal account, so far this has worked well'. Amelia then delivers the course over six weeks with content being delivered three times a week. Students are able to upload their work to a private area where Amelia will personally critique it.

When it comes to promotion Amelia's blog plays a crucial role in driving sales for her courses:

I have a blog dedicated to art, with information about art but also my own life and experiences too. I love other blogs and sites where you get a real flavour of the person behind the work and hearing their own ups and downs. I found this helpful, and so as well as my successes I wanted to re-count the genuine challenges I have faced up to today, doing what I do and being a mother and carer. From the blog and my own art website I advertise that I run the experimental art e-course.

Amelia has also tried a number of other online marketing strategies.

I spend money advertising on some key art blogs with large amounts of traffic. Some of these involve sponsor spotlights which are great ways to 'talk about' a product and, in my case, the course. I also rely on word of mouth – happy customers putting logos on their sites and telling others about it and encouraging them to do it also – lots of participants have come this way. That's why I always have a feedback form at the end to capture people's thoughts and testimonials .... Interviews are good too, as are guest posts – but I do not do too many of these. Basically the key I feel is in having good content and being genuinely passionate about what I do.

Since starting her own eCourses Amelia has become a real advocate for the format, she says:

I chose e-courses because I know as a mother there are times when getting childcare and paying for it too can be challenging – e-courses allow people to go without childcare and do the course from the comfort of home when little ones are sleeping or at school! I am a real people's person and love the community element of running courses and meeting all the lovely interesting people across the globe and sharing what we all know together – I have met great people from doing the courses and I absolutely love it! I am passionate about art and I wrote a course that wasn't 'box-ticking' or what an institution wanted me to do. I wrote it from the bottom of my heart, from the angle that we are all creative and can do art. By writing my own entire course I could put in exactly what I would like to do myself and what I observed many grownups would like to do and by doing it through an on-line course it is less intimidating – no-one else has to see unless one chooses to show it!

TAKE ACTION

- Consider your knowledge and skills and start researching possible niches. Don't have the knowledge? Consider partnering with someone who does!
- Carry out the appropriate market research
- Found a viable niche? Start planning your eCourse content
- Focus on building your perceived expertise and following (see Chapter 3)
- Write/create six weeks of content
- Sell your eCourse!
- Create further content and consider complementary products that you can sell to your members

Profitable niches include anything to do with health, finding love and dating, making money and being successful. You will be able to find many more ideas once you look at your own skills, knowledge and interests and start researching online.

5 Creating Your Products: eBooks

In Chapter 3, which focuses on building your profile as an expert, we mentioned that, 'writing a book does an enormous amount to build your authority'. There are many advantages to being a published author and ePublishing puts this within almost anyone's reach. If you have great ideas that solve problems for people in a particular niche market and you can put those ideas into words, you are on your way to creating an eBook.

There are various ways to create an eBook – you can do it all yourself, use a 'co-publisher' who has technical knowledge of the publishing process and will work with you to publish your book, or go for a more traditional contract with a publisher who issues the book in print and as an eBook. Later in this chapter we will assess the risks and benefits of these options.

Perhaps most importantly for anyone who wants to make money online, an eBook is a great example of a scalable product. You can sell unlimited numbers of eBooks without increasing your inputs, either of time or money.

WHY WRITE AN EBOOK

- To raise your profile
- Because it is scalable

- Because you avoid swapping 'time for money'
- Because it can be sold by affiliates
- Because it suits almost any niche
- It has low production costs
- It can cope with time sensitive and up-to-the-minute topics
- It allows your followers to buy your expertise

WHAT NOT TO EXPECT FROM YOUR EBOOK

Do not expect that your first eBook will make your fortune. It might, but it is rare to get an overnight runaway success. In fact, you might even decide to give away your first eBook to help build your reputation and grow your mailing list. Instead, look at your first eBook as a test run or learning experience. Do not let this put you off though: once you have written a few eBooks and have perfected a marketing strategy you will find that the sales come in for each book in a steady flow and make a valuable contribution to your income.

Case Study: Joe Gregory of Bookshaker

www.bookshaker.com

Joe Gregory is an independent publisher and author of over twenty books including *The Wealthy Author*. Read how he moved from exchanging time for money to making a full-time income from running his independent publishing company, and the critical role that his first eBook played.

Back in the 1990s, Joe owned and ran a busy marketing business with ten members of staff, but realized that he wasn't in business to be a boss. Joe says,

I started my own business when I was 19. The business was growing, we had big premises in Birmingham and a good turnover. But I wasn't a good boss, I was always torn between being friends with people and getting jobs done. I was in business with my sister at the time, and we had a moment where we sat down and looked at our ideal day. We realised we didn't want to sell time for money. We had lots of clients relying on us, and in reality it felt like we were employees, but of lots of different companies. We weren't free in the way that lots of people imagine when they start their own business. We didn't really have the time freedom and that was one of our big goals.

Joe and his sister, Debbie Jenkins, took action to restructure the way they worked:

We systematically reduced everything we had to do, and created 'lean marketing', getting maximum out for minimum effort. We wrote the process down and turned it into a book called *The Gorillas Want Bananas*. We wanted to start selling the book rather than our time. We could give clients the way to keep their businesses small and powerful without doing things like advertising. That book sold really well. It started as an eBook. At the time in 1999/2000 it was still possible to sell eBooks for £100 or £200. Ours cost £97 and sold well. We then set up our publishing company and published 37 books in the first couple of years. Now I publish around 20 books a year and own a number of imprints.

One of the great things about eBooks is that you have exclusivity. If the information is packaged well and people really want it you can set the price. And you can set it a lot higher than you could for a hard copy book. Nowadays people expect more value added, some coaching or some teleseminars with the book but I still think if you package your information well, maybe calling it a course, you can keep the exclusivity. Of course, if you are looking for maximum reach, you can sell your book to read on Kindle or via Smashwords. You are in a known product price area where people will say, 'I only pay £4' or 'I only pay $10' and then the exclusivity is gone. That massively changes the dynamics. You have to sell a lot more products to make your profits. If the eBook is there to get more business for your main business, then I would suggest getting it as wide and far as you can. Even sell it for as little as £1 on Kindle just to get lots of people reading your message. Then they will become fans of you and you may have something bigger to sell them, whether it is a teleseminar series or DVDs or audios. This makes your eBook a front end way to get lots of leads.

Joe advises,

> If the only product that you have got is an eBook, really work on its exclusivity, do not allow it to be sold here, there and everywhere. Make it something that is exclusive to your website. Have a plan to have lots of books that can follow that. Not very long ago we were selling The Amazon Best Seller Plan for £50, because we kept it exclusive. That was selling well. You can make a lot more selling 100 books at £50 than 1000 books at £5, get there more quickly. At the starting stage if you need cash flow you need a high value, high price product.

Joe's own situation has changed now he has around 100 books in print. He explains,

> Now I publish on Smashwords and for Kindle and in print. Because I have a critical mass of books, just over 100 books

that I have authored or published, I have a very nice income coming from those books, which is generally passive. I do not have to do a lot. Amazon fulfils the orders for print books, Kindle books download automatically. All of these sources, they just send me money and a report of what was sold there. I then do the calculations to pay my authors. It is a very nice position to be in, but actually to generate enough cash flow I would suggest you need at least 20 books selling reasonably well, a couple of hundred copies a month, to make that happen. Otherwise you won't replace a regular job income. With the other model, if you sell a book for £50, say you want to earn £1000 a month, you do not need to sell a lot of books. You can concentrate on social media marketing using sites like Facebook to sell the odd copy here and there until you have built a critical mass.

THE PURPOSE OF YOUR EBOOK

Why are you writing an eBook? Be clear about your purpose from the start and you will be far more likely to achieve your goals. Here are three possible aims for your eBook:

To grow your list

An eBook is a great way to grow the list of people who have opted in to receive email marketing from you. You offer the eBook as a sign-up incentive to join your list. This sort of free eBook is the ideal item to offer at the top of your product funnel, drawing people in by giving them a taster of what you offer, and leading them on to buy items of increasing value. If you are creating your first eBook, why not start here? Do not be tempted, though, to skimp on offering great content: a free eBook does not have to be lengthy but if it is the first time people come into contact with you and what you offer you want it to include some really outstanding examples of how you can help them.

To help you find clients

This is a logical follow-on from the first purpose. Your eBook can be a valuable way to find clients for coaching or other one-to-one or group work. Address the types of problems that possible clients face and existing clients want to be addressed. Put in lots of value: do not worry about deterring people who might read your eBook and then not need your help. This type of person is in a small minority and would have been likely to solve their own problems anyway. Instead, include great case studies, examples and testimonials of people who you *have* worked with and how they have triumphed.

For sale

An eBook can fill in the second level of your product funnel: a low cost item available to many, without extra input from you. This is the ideal way to allow hundreds and thousands of people to share your expertise and get help from you to solve the particular problem they are encountering, even if they can't work with you one to one. You can maximize sales of an eBook by making sure it appears on Amazon and other online book stores and by making it available to affiliates to promote. Alternatively, you may want to make your eBook significantly more expensive and only available on an exclusive basis. This is one route that Joe Gregory has followed with success. He advises, 'Because people now have gadgets and devices and can search for stuff, you can have a small niche and have the potential to be found. That's called "the long tail". If you have something unique keep it exclusive.'

Whatever your pricing, include lots of great material in your eBook: people are paying to have your expertise available via their desktop.

CREATING AN EBOOK

If you have never written an eBook before, the very idea can seem daunting, so here are some quick tips to help you get underway.

Gather together material you have written already

If you have ever written an article or a blog post, you could be on your way to creating your eBook. Take some time to collate information that you have created already and note down obvious gaps or additions that occur to you as you do so. Depending on the way you work you might want to print out articles, or paste them into a file. With any luck you will be pleasantly surprised by the amount of potential material you have.

Ask your followers

Next, spend some time noting down topics you often get asked about. If you want, you could mind map all the possible topics you could write on. Alternatively, if you have people on your email list already, send out a request asking them what topics they would like further information about from you. You can post a similar request for your blog readers. In placing these requests, you do not need to commit to fulfilling them all in an eBook: some ideas may simply end up as blog posts or the topic for your next newsletter. Getting this feedback from your followers is an invaluable part of your research stage.

Do your market research

As we mentioned in Chapter 4, market research is an essential part of developing your ideas for your eBook. Re-read the 'Factors to consider' section of Chapter 4 and see how they apply to your possible eBook topics. Take time to scan other websites, look for other eCourses and eBooks and browse through Amazon to see what else is out there on the topic. You are ideally looking for a gap in the market where you can offer something new that is not already covered in book format. Coach and online entrepreneur Karen Skidmore says,

> Focus on something that your customers are wanting. Do not go through all the heartache and struggle of getting the platform and payments set up without checking you have done something people want to buy. Make sure that you have content that you *know* people would spend money on. Do not just get together a group of girlfriends: do detailed market research into exactly what people would want to spend money on before you create the content.

Plan and structure

Your next step is to bring together your existing materials, the questions your followers want answered and your market research. Can you find a topic that you are ready to write on and combine it with a gap in the market that your followers want to know about? If so, you could be on to a winning topic for your eBook. Now is the time to plan your eBook in more detail.

Here are some of the essential questions to answer when creating your plan for your eBook:

- What is unique about this eBook?
- Why should people buy it?
- Who is the eBook for?
- What will people learn from the eBook?
- What are the benefits they will get from reading it?

Next, work out topics for your chapters and list them. Under each chapter topic, list the sub-topics you will cover. At this stage you could estimate the word count for each chapter and section, which can give you some targets to work towards. Use some of your previous articles to help you estimate. To help you, a slim paperback could be as little as 25,000 words while a chunkier book could be anything from 55,000 to 90,000 words; eBooks are not confined by traditional print publishing boundaries and can be just a few thousand words long if you are giving them away, up to full book length.

Case Study: Allison Marlowe – Creating an eBook in a month

www.allisonmarlowe.com

Allison Marlowe is a dynamic coach who works with female entrepreneurs. She belongs to a mastermind group, where members work together to achieve their goals. At one of these groups members were talking about author status, and how it gets you closer to the top of the pyramid of power and profit. Allison explains,

> The group leader challenged us to get a book published by the end of the month – just a couple of weeks away. I love challenges so I said I had to do it. I wanted to complete the challenge and I wanted to learn just what the process would

be all about. Was it within my capability, could I put the words together? I then had to find a topic. I asked myself, 'What is my story?' I spoke to my networking group, Hampshire Winning Women, and we came up with the idea of a tip booklet. We talked about the things we wished we'd known at the beginning, things we'd wasted time and money over. It was a great idea, but I decided that this wasn't the book for the challenge, but one I had to do later. I then met some members from the mastermind group the following Wednesday, and we decided to collaborate on an eBook. We all had our stories of how we'd got started, how we'd over-come obstacles: we'd create a book for all those women who are being held back by feeling 'I am not good enough.' Collaborating made the process easier and more manageable. I sat for two afternoons over the Christmas Holidays and just wrote. I didn't edit: I just told my story. I was amazed at the things that were coming out. I wasn't intentionally writing to inspire, I just laid my story bare. It is in that way that people can get to know the true you. If it inspires just one person, then I know that I have done a fabulous job.

Then the nine of us set up a closed Facebook group. We had lots of conversations about how we were going to publish. We knew that, for every print book, more and more people are downloading eBooks to Kindle ... something like 30 eBooks for every print book. I had had it in my mind that this had to be a physical book, something we could publish on Lulu.com, but when I discovered this fact, an eBook made sense. It was the quickest way too. We published following guidelines from Amazon – totally step by step. We listed the authors, created the blurb for the back of the book and one of the members took the lead on formatting, fonts etc to get it into print. Now we are on a mini mission to get that book out there. The beautiful thing about having an eBook that I didn't realise, when it is being promoted via Amazon, people do not even have to have a Kindle – people can print the book out too.

Allison says, 'I was very fearful, but if your message is bigger than your fear, just do it. Look at creating an eBook as your opportunity. If you have something that will resonate with and help other people, you have a duty to create your eBook.'

PUBLISHERS AND EBOOKS

Once you have your plan for content, you also need to work out how you will get the book to press. Find out about the various ways to create an eBook, assess the risks and benefits of these options and learn what you need to know for each option.

Getting your eBook to press: self-publishing options

More and more people are self-publishing eBooks. Murielle Maupoint from Live It Publishing explains that, when self-publishing,

You take responsibility for everything to do with your book – writing, editing, typesetting, cover design, printing, marketing, sales and distribution. For the control freaks out there, this can be a very good option as you have full control and you get a greater margin for every book sold. And for some this works very well – *In Search of Excellence* was initially self-published and sold over 25,000 copies in its first year before it was picked up by a mainstream publisher.

If this sounds like the option for you, here is some guidance from Joe Gregory who has written and published around twenty of his own books and over a hundred including those from other authors through his business www.bookshaker.com. If you are creating your first eBook, the first skill Gregory suggests you master is to be able to word process your book and create a pdf or Portable Document Format.

I have used Microsoft Word pretty much exclusively, even when creating print books. It is only recently that I have bought and started to use Adobe InDesign. Now you can use all sorts of things to get your book looking good. You can download OpenOffice, which is a perfectly good word processing package. It has a lot of features that allow you to make a very nice looking eBook at no cost. It is very user friendly.

Then, you simply need to create a pdf. The advantage is that it will look pretty much the same on everyone's computer. It is widely supported and works across all sorts of devices. I am currently reading a pdf on my Kindle: it is not perfect but it works fine. If you buy Acrobat you can password protect it, giving you a level of security. You can limit people from printing and reprinting the book.

You can find free pdf creators online, you will find pdf conversion as one of the functions on up-to-date versions of Word or you can use Adobe Acrobat.

Gregory continues:

If your goal is to sell lots of books as a lead generator you can set up for Kindle with just a Word formatted file. If you go to dtp.amazon.co.uk you will find the information and downloads about how to make your Word file work. You upload the file and the site turns it into a Kindle-friendly format for you. There is no need for Acrobat or pdfs. Kindle has apps for all sorts of devices so I think it is a great place to start. People trust Amazon a lot more readily and might buy from there if they won't buy from your newly set up website.

You may also want to check out www.smashwords.com, an online publishing portal that allows independent authors and publishers to publish, distribute and sell eBooks to a worldwide audience at the largest eBook retailers. Gregory adds, 'Kindle outstrips what I get from Smashwords as it fits in so well with Amazon, but I think Smashwords is where the future is. Otherwise you have to pay people to get your book into the right format for different readers.'

E-junkie is another option: Erica Douglas explains,

> I created my eBook from an eCourse I had developed. I simply took the eLessons and turned them into mini chapters. Turning the eBook into a pdf was a simple process and then I paid someone £40 to create a front cover and spruce up the book with some pictures. After doing a bit of research I found that the easiest way for me to sell my eBook was via E-junkie. I simply had to upload the eBook file and then checkout and payment is dealt with via them. The funds are deposited directly into my PayPal. E-junkie allows me to sell copies of my eBook around the clock and they only charge me a monthly fee of a few dollars. It is a great solution for someone just starting out in online business.

There are other sites like this: do some research online if you want to explore further options.

Costs of self-publishing an eBook

Creating an eBook can be a genuinely low cost exercise, but if you have a small budget you can create something much more professional than you can alone. Do not skimp on editing and proofreading: if at all possible avoid doing this yourself. Joe

Gregory explains the importance of having a well edited eBook. 'As far as quality goes, people will judge a book on grammar. The job of an editor adds a lot of value but is not necessarily visible.' The same applies to proofreading: no one notices a well proofed book, but plenty of people will be deterred from using your services or buying further products if they spot spelling and grammatical errors.

There are plenty of freelance editors and proofreaders to be found online. Visit www.sfep.org.uk for lists of members of the Society for Editors and Proofreaders, plus current suggested rates. Get quotes using sites like eLance, Odesk or PeoplePerHour to find freelancers if you do not have contacts of your own. Joe Gregory has a suggestion that can help if you are on a tight budget: 'Editors can charge a lot of money. I have a small panel of editors that I work with whom I have negotiated that they work in collaboration for, say, 10% to 20% of the overall profit of the book as an ongoing royalty. That helps them develop their passive income. Many editors won't work this way, though.'

When planning your eBook, you may need help with:

- Editing
- Proofreading
- Cover design
- Inside layout

At the planning stage, start building contacts, checking out examples of their work and getting quotes from the freelancers you may need to create an attractive professional eBook.

Printing your self-published eBook

You may decide that you need print copies of your self-published eBook, and there are lots of options to help you do this. First, though, make sure you have a minimum word count of 15,000 words, which would make a slim paperback. And, you need to get quotes for the cost of printing, and have the space to store your books. Then, watch out for a number of pitfalls, as explained by Murielle Maupoint from Live It Publishing: 'It is not cost-effective without printing in volume and with that you then need the storage and distribution channels to sell them in their thousands. It will be of no surprise to you then that many great self-published books sit unsold in authors' garages gathering dust and damp!' What is more, trends show that more people are buying eBooks every day: Joe Gregory explains, 'One of our authors is outselling his print books with an eBook two to one, averaging around 500 sales a month. If you can get that repeatable month on month it makes a nice passive income base.'

With that advice, you may decide to stick to eBooks! However, if you have got a great cover design, have had help with editing and proofreading and know that you are ready to put the time into promoting your print book, there are many print on demand publishers who allow you to print anything from a single copy of your book up to thousands of copies. Note that you will find the cost per copy diminishes as the number you order increases. Just type 'print on demand' into a search engine to find companies that supply this service. I have had some of my own books printed in batches of 500 or 1,000, knowing that I have created a ready niche audience who want to buy. I have sold these successfully, made a profit, won awards and greatly increased my business profile within my niche as a result of bringing out the print book, which I then followed with an eBook version. I find my print books sell well when I speak at live events and can make these events much more profitable.

Getting your eBook to press: traditional publishing

When most people consider writing a book, they first think of approaching a mainstream publisher. Murielle Maupoint explains the benefits and issues of mainstream publishing,

You receive an advance on royalties cheque and the publisher will deal with all aspects of designing, editing, printing, marketing, selling and distributing your book. The downside invariably is that you lose a certain amount of control and you will only get a very small percentage for royalties on each book sold. Whilst this model is a great way to get your work known by the masses, the truth is that the vast majority of manuscripts sent to mainstream publishers are rejected.

Nowadays, if you do get a contract from a traditional publisher, it is extremely likely to contain options for eBook publishing. Do explore exactly what the publisher practises: some are more proactive about actually taking up the eBook option than others. Get guidance on contracts from the Society of Authors, and find lists of publishers and the sectors they cover within the *Writers' and Artists' Yearbook*.

Getting your eBook to press: co-publishing

Co-publishing is an option that has grown rapidly in the last few years. Authors link up with independent publishers who tend not to pay an advance, but will assist the author to get their eBook to press and will have distribution channels and printing arrangements already set up. Murielle Maupoint explains how it can help you:

> Co-publishing or partnership publishing bridges the benefits of both mainstream publishing and self-publishing. Partnership Publishing does exactly what it says on the tin – it works in partnership with the author to get works published, sold and distributed. This means that the author receives the professional expertise, guidance and royalties that you would expect with a mainstream publisher whilst also retaining literary control of their works and massively reducing the financial

investment linked with self-publishing. Essentially, in this model the author and publisher share the cost and rewards of getting the works print ready, published and distributed. The author can therefore focus on what he or she does best – writing the book and promoting it, and the publisher does what it does best, which is to turn the book into a sellable product and manage all the processes to do with editing, proofreading, design, printing, legality, sales and distribution. It is easy to see how partnership publishing is a popular option for most new authors – offering them the best of both worlds.

SELLING BOOKS AND EBOOKS

So, by now, you should have a fair idea of where you are going to start with your eBook. You might be at the planning stage, or maybe you have already got some content down on paper. Whatever stage you are at, make some time to work on the most important element in getting an eBook out into the world. Some people might say that this is the content, and excellent content contributes to the success of an eBook. However, the most important part of planning your eBook is to plan the promotion. Without great promotion, an eBook can have amazing content yet no readers. Published authors with the backing of mainstream publishers still find that more often than not they are responsible for the bulk of their own marketing. So, how do you spread the word about your book?

If you have been putting into practice everything you read in Chapter 3 about building your profile as an expert and finding followers you will find this is critical to all promotion. You should have a good list of followers to get your launch off to a great start. Then think what you can do to start building a relationship with these followers. One great example of this is contained within Yaro Starak's Membership Mastermind eCourse where he offers, as a bonus, an eBook containing the thirty-five emails he used when launching Blog Mastermind. Yes, that's right, thirty-five emails. If you read the emails, you will see that they are not at all salesy: instead what they do is take the reader along with Yaro in his journey to build the course. Over a number of months he shares his progress, the ups, downs and delays, and in the process gets the readers really inspired about the content he is creating.

Now, you do not have to create thirty-five emails as a matter of course, but what you do need to consider is how you will use email, Twitter, your website and blog to draw people in so that they desire your eBook or course. If you are in a hurry to get on to this part of making money online, you might want to skip on to Chapter 11 where we lay out strategies. Right now, though, just start making your plans. Go back to those essential questions we listed earlier in this chapter:

- What is unique about this eBook?
- Why should people buy it?
- Who is the eBook for?
- What will people learn from the eBook?
- What are the benefits they will get from reading it?

These questions will form the heart of your marketing plan. Then start jotting down your ideas about how you can get your readers and followers to follow your journey as you create your product, how you can get them to need, want and desire what you are offering and truly understand how this eBook could solve their particular problem in a way that no other product can.

TAKE ACTION

What action do you need to take now?

1. Decide whether an eBook is the right product for you to make money online

2. Create a plan for your book, and do some market research to see if there is a need for an eBook in this niche

3. Set yourself some goals and deadlines for getting the content written

4. Get networking to build a list of followers who are interested in your niche *and* to find possible editors, proofreaders or designers to assist with your book

There is a lot more about the technicalities of publishing and promoting an eBook that we can't include in this chapter. If this sounds like the way you'd like to start making money online, read *The Wealthy Author* by Joe Gregory and Debbie Jenkins. If you are keen to start planning promotion for your eBook and other online products, there is more on this topic in Chapter 11. For further help, read *A Guide to Promoting Your Business* and *DIY Marketing: The Essential Guide*, both by Antonia Chitty.

6 Make it, Market it

I n this chapter we are going to briefly look away from eProd-
ucts and focus on the many ways in which you can sell
handmade and artisanal goods over the internet. Trading
handcrafted goods has become a growing market online with
dedicated marketplaces such as Etsy and Folksy, making buying
and selling as simple as trading at your local market. Of course,
over the internet you do not need to worry about the weather!

If you enjoy creating handcrafted goods such as cards, soft
furnishings, clothes or candles the internet is a great way to find
a market for your products, and a global market at that! Many
struggling artists have found their '1,000 true fans' online and
now make a respectable living doing what they love. Being able
to turn a hobby into a good income stream is a dream for many
people. If this sounds like you then read on to see if you can make
that dream a reality.

Case Study: Jo Thorpe of Jo Thorpe Mosaic

www.shizzleshop.com

Jo Thorpe is a mosaic artist based in East London. She stumbled
upon the idea of creating and selling scrabble tile pendants by
chance. Jo wanted a 'J' scrabble pendant for herself but says she
couldn't buy one for love nor money as 'J's were so popular.
Before moving house Jo had spotted scrabble tiles lying on the

floor of the garage and she collected them all up. Luckily for her there was a 'J' amongst the tiles and with a little help from her Dad and his drill her first pendant was created. It wasn't long before friends and family were asking Jo to create tiles for them, then friends of friends and so on ...

Demand for the scrabble pendants grew and soon a friend of Jo's was helping her create and market the pendants. 'We sent every stylist from all the main magazines a necklace as early Christmas presents and *Fabulous, The Observer Magazine & Grazia* included us in their Christmas present guides.' Sales of the scrabble pendants grew substantially and in the run up to Christmas over 600 pendants were sold. The ladies also sold them at festivals after Jo used one of her contacts to secure a pitch.

Since then Jo and her unique necklaces have been featured in the *Independent* and she's utilizing social media to further raise the profile of her product. Jo now has a presence on Twitter and Facebook but admits to being bad at tweeting! Jo also has her own blog where people can contact her to make purchases. She'll be expanding her range to include gold necklaces as part of her Etsy shop. Jo says that marketing via the internet has been 'easy, cheap and far reaching'. Jo's advice to those just starting out is 'keep coming up with new ideas and be creative, use your contacts and create opportunities and do fun things like craft markets'.

One of the keys to success is establishing whether your hobby could become a viable business proposition. In this section we will look at things to consider before starting up your handcrafts business and how to ensure that you make a reasonable profit.

WHY SELL YOUR HANDMADE PRODUCTS?

If you are keen to create your own income streams, selling your handmade crafts can be a good way to get started. Not only will you be able to spend your time doing something that you love but you will be able to make some money too. The internet has made it easy for you to find customers for your goods with sites like eBay, Etsy, Folksy and Amazon acting as global marketplaces. We will go into more detail about these sites later in the chapter but, for now, consider your own hobby, whether it has the potential to create an income for you and whether turning your hobby into a business is something you'd want to do.

At this point some of you will be shouting 'Of course I want to spend time being paid to do my hobby', but think for a moment about whether your hobby would still be as enjoyable if you had to spend eight hours a day doing it to make ends meet.

THINGS TO CONSIDER BEFORE TRYING TO TURN YOUR HOBBY INTO A BUSINESS

1. Is my hobby something that someone would pay for?

Finding out whether people other than your friends and family will pay for your products is key to establishing whether you have a viable business proposition. The best way to find out whether people would buy your product is to *ask*. However, avoid asking family or friends as nine times out of ten they will tell you what you want to hear. Set up a basic poll using survey software like Survey Monkey and put it on a forum or your blog. This will allow people to confidentially let you know if your idea has legs. You can spread the word about surveys via Facebook, Twitter and other social media in a fast and effective way.

Your market research shouldn't stop there; if it looks like your products have potential then you need to do some more in depth research. First you need to establish who your target market is.

For example, are you aiming at 'young affluent males' or 'middle aged females who enjoy cookery'?

Second, find out where your target market congregate online or offline and find a way of surveying them about the specifics of your product or service. You need to find out how much they would pay, how often they would buy etc. You will need this kind of information to establish whether the market is large enough for your product or service to provide you with a steady income stream and ongoing sales.

2. Can my hobby become a viable business? Can it be profitable?

It is fun making handmade cards but can it be a profitable business? Can you produce enough cards per hour to provide a decent hourly rate? You need to bring together:

- your costings – how much it costs to produce each card
- your market research – how much buyers are willing to pay
- time analysis – how long each card takes to produce

Do the figures stack up? As much as you might love the idea of spending your days making beautiful handmade cards, if it is not profitable then you are wasting your time. This analysis should be applied when you are in the process of researching and evaluating any business idea.

Unfortunately this is where many businesses selling hand-crafted goods slip up as it is usually very time consuming to create the products and so this drives the price up to the point where consumers are not willing to pay. Do not fall into the trap of creating a business that does not make any money. If you can sell a handmade card for £3 and it costs you £3 to produce then you do not have a viable business venture. Remember to factor things like equipment, lighting and heating into your costs, and add the cost of premises if you need them.

3. Is my hobby scalable?

If it is a business you are looking to build then you need to consider whether your 'hobby' can be automated in any way, and whether you can outsource any aspects of the service or production. If the answer to the above is yes, you then need to consider whether the cost of doing so still makes for a profitable business. Let's say you can sell your cards for £3 and you can produce six an hour. That's £18. If you take off the cost of producing each card (£2 per card) then your profit is £6. If you then employ someone at £6 per hour to produce the cards you are making £0. Therefore, your business is limited to the amount of hours you can work on it yourself. If you are simply happy to be earning a living doing your hobby and making 'some' money from it then this is an avenue worth pursuing, but go into it with your eyes open and your expectations set appropriately.

4. Will it still be a hobby when it is paying the bills?

The final consideration is whether, when you are doing your hobby as a 'job' or it is your business, you will still enjoy it in the same way. For example, you enjoy spending a Sunday afternoon creating beautiful handmade cards for family and friends. Now imagine you are doing that 9am–3pm every day to make money – will it still be as enjoyable?

So, those are some questions to ask yourself before turning your hobby into a business. Read on for more guidance on developing your products, finding ideas for products and making them sell.

WHAT TO SELL

What you are going to sell may be obvious to you if you already have an established hobby or you have stumbled across a desirable product like Jo, but remember: just because you make it does not mean people want to buy it. Try selling a few of your products via eBay to test the market. If you do not already have an idea of what to sell then refer back to Chapter 1, Finding Your Niche.

When thinking about what handcrafted items to make it is worth considering the motivation for buying such products. Usually these products are bought as 'luxury' or 'feel good' purchases. The good news is that consumers are less focused on price when making such purchases, which are often impulsive, so the staging and photographing of your goods must be excellent. The bad news is that you are tapping into the consumers' desires. They do not need your product so you have to make them want it. This can be a difficult thing to do. Consumers face endless buying choices every day. What is going to make them buy *your* product?

Look for gaps in the market and create something completely unique. If you can come up with something that is truly desirable and you are the 'first and original' then this is a great route to success as you can also charge a premium. Look at products that already sell well and consider how you can adjust or improve upon them.

Follow fashions. Many products come in and out of fashion. Certain scents will be all the rage before the next big thing supersedes it. At times of Royal celebration the Union Jack becomes very popular and we see a plethora of Union Jack inspired soft furnishings and posters. Think about upcoming events and what might be the next fashion trend. Alternatively target classic trends that are timeless and go for the extreme luxury end of the market, where the most profit can be made.

WHERE TO SELL

There are a number of online marketplaces for your goods. In this section we will look at some of the most popular. It may be that you will need to try each of the different sites to see which one converts best for you. You may find a blend of two or three works well. Do not limit yourself to one outlet until you have done some testing.

Etsy

Etsy is an online marketplace specializing in handmade and vintage products. Products on Etsy range from candles to accessories and soft furnishings. Vintage items are those categorized as being twenty years old or older. Etsy's mission statement is 'to enable people to make a living making things, and to reconnect makers with buyers'. Their ultimate aim is to bring buyers and sellers together and encourage people to buy and use handmade. They have a completely different emphasis to sites like eBay and Amazon, which are among the largest online auction and trading sites in the world but where the focus is not on handmade goods. Etsy's image is very much handcrafted, classic, back to basics, and when choosing your online marketplace you should consider the perception you wish to create for your brand and products.

Case Study: Rachel Lucie of Rachel Lucie Jewellery

www.rachellucie.co.uk

I signed up for Etsy in July 2008, and created a shop in September of that year. I only started making jewellery in February 2008, so I really was just testing the water. There were no orders at all for the first month, but in November and December I got a few sales, and so was quite happy. My second Christmas was great. Fast forward to now, and Etsy is a very hard place to sell. Being a UK seller does put you at a disadvantage in terms of pricing, as the cost of materials (and the variety) seems to be much better in the US.

Etsy does have a shop local feature, which is great, and half of my sales are actually from UK buyers who have probably found me this way. I think another problem with Etsy is that it has more than doubled in terms of sellers in the last 3 years – there are over a million and a half now, and over 7,000,000 products! A lot of them are jewellery, too. It has been increasingly hard to get seen and make the sales I need to make it pay. There are some golden rules to getting sales which I do not have time to do, and do not suit the way I work nowadays. These are:

- if possible, list something new every day or certainly every couple of days
- renew listed items regularly so they appear as newly listed
- take part in the forums several times a day
- have giveaways, discounts and contests

I have also been in some treasury teams which hope to get you exposure on the front page, although front page exposure in itself does not necessarily lead to sales (but you get masses of views for your shop).

Etsy has been a great place to learn from, though. The culture is open and friendly, and generally I feel I have made lots of friends there. People are helpful, which was invaluable when I first started selling online, and give advice. It is a great community. I think, in a way, for the average seller, this might be the downfall, it is kind of a great place to be for the home crafter, but not necessarily somewhere to make your living. There are obvious exceptions, and some sellers do very well there and have fantastically placed products for the market. We would all do well to learn from them!

I have had my own website for just over a year now,

although I have only been with my current ecommerce provider with the new website since October, and I have been very pleased with how it is going. I certainly am getting sales, with some repeat sales, too. I am particularly excited when a sale on my own website comes through as this means that not only did someone find my site and like my work, but they also trusted my site, too. This is a massive deal online. Anyone can set up a website, and people are understandably very conscious of possible fraud. For someone to see and trust my little brand is an enormous compliment. I have certainly had many more sales on my own site than Etsy in the past few months. It is great to have my own site to direct people too, also. I have made it how I like, and have a lot of control of the design and all of the content. The package I am on has allowed me to make most of the changes myself, which suits me as I am a bit of a secret geek! I sell on other gift sites online, too, with my biggest seller of all being Notonthehighstreet.

Folksy

Folksy is a British-based online marketplace for handcrafted goods with its headquarters in Sheffield. It differs from Etsy in that it does not allow vintage items. Folksy's aim is to 'showcase the work of independent UK artists, designers and crafters'. Folksy has grown in popularity since its launch in 2007 and is now a leading online UK marketplace for handcrafted goods.

Case Study: Diane Clarke of Peggy's Knits

www.peggyscollection.com

Diane's business Peggy's Knits grew out of her passion for crafting. After she'd had children, she found that turning her passion for crafting into a business was a viable option and Peggy's Knits was born. Diane sells via both Folksy and Etsy. She says:

Folksy is a UK based website and I have sold a lot of items on there. It is great for the 'made in the UK' brand. Etsy is an international based website and I have made sales in the USA etc on there too, but not sold as much. Folksy does not have as many sellers as Etsy does so there is a lot more choice on Etsy.

The success of Diane's business relies heavily on the promotion she does. She has found Twitter, Facebook and blogging all useful ways to promote her business.

DaWanda

DaWanda is the new handcrafted marketplace on the block. Launched in 2009 they bring together the online marketplace with social media, forums and blogs. Their aim is to bring buyers and artists/crafters together and take the provenance trend to a new level. Buyers can get to know the people behind the products, learn about the products and then buy them.

MISI

Launched in 2008 by a keen crafter, MISI, which stands for 'Make It Sell It', has grown to 3,000 sellers and 75,000 page views, proving that the market for buying and selling handcrafted products is still very buoyant.

Selling via your own site

Another way to sell is via your own site. This can be as simple as a blog with a shopping cart. Having your own site has additional advantages like having more space to talk about your products, how they are created, their provenance etc. Blogs also rank really well in search engines so could provide you with a steady stream of visitors interested in the products you create. Refer back to Chapter 2 on how to start your own blog and read on for things to consider when selling via your own site, and via big craft sites too.

Terms and conditions

When choosing an online marketplace to trade from always check the terms and conditions first. Do not forget to check the fees for selling; these vary across the sites. If selling via your own site you will need terms and conditions too.

Postage and packaging

Remember to factor in the costs of postage and packaging when pricing your goods.

Delivery

Consider which delivery channels you will use and how you will organize this. If you have your own site you need to give information about times and costs for delivery; if you are selling via a big craft site they may have specific requirements for you to meet.

SALES: YOUR BIGGEST CHALLENGE

Marketing a business and continuing to drive sales is a challenge for many small business owners, particularly those who would prefer to spend their time creating handcrafted goods rather than creating and implementing marketing strategies! However, if you want to continue making sales then a bit of marketing is a necessity. The internet provides a number of low cost and free ways to market your business that can be fun *and* allow you to express your creativity. There are details of some of these below.

Facebook

It is simple to create a Facebook page for your business and it gives your fans a focal point. Start by setting up your page and getting the three Fs (family, friends and fans) to 'like' your page. Every time your page is 'liked' you appear in that person's Facebook stream, which means all their friends are made aware of your business. The more 'likes' you can get the more sets of eyes that see your business. Update your page regularly with new products, photos and promotions. Link back to your site often to encourage sales.

Twitter

Twitter is a great tool for promoting your business and engaging with your customers. An account is easy to set up. Pick a memorable name that reflects what your business does and upload a photo. If you do not include a photo people may think that you are a spammer. People will start following you as you start tweeting but to get yourself started use the search function to find people to follow that you know or think you would be interested in. Drive sales by occasionally linking to discounts and products or highlighting promotions.

YouTube

Get creative with video for the best results. Create short how to or demonstration clips that you can upload to your own YouTube channel. Do not forget to promote your videos on Twitter, Facebook and, if you have one, your blog. Editing software like Camtasia can add a professional look to your videos.

A blog

Blogging can be great fun and appeals to many creative types. Setting up a blog is not as complex or expensive as you may think. Buying a domain name and having a tech person install WordPress can be done for under £200 (the free version has strict rules on selling/advertising). You can then promote your products in the content of your blog as well as in the sidebar. See Chapter 2 for more details on blogging.

YOUR MARKETING PLAN

Create a plan to keep you on track with your marketing efforts. Set aside a bit of time first thing to do one piece of marketing. Once you are in the habit of marketing your business you will find that it becomes a habit and you may even begin to enjoy it. Effective marketing requires compound effort; you need to be consistent and persistent before you begin to see results. By constantly getting your message out there it won't be long before you become well known in your niche for whatever it is that you create or provide. The ultimate aim is for people to think of you as soon as they think of the product you create.

7 Selling Other People's Products

Selling other people's products online is known as affiliate marketing. The idea is that you promote and sell someone else's products usually for a percentage share of the price of the goods. There are affiliate marketing opportunities across the internet for every niche you can think of, whatever your hobby, passion or area of expertise. Be warned: as more people learn about affiliate marketing, niches are becoming crowded and increasingly competitive so move fast and choose your niche carefully.

Affiliate marketing as an income stream has a number of advantages. It is a quick way to start earning if you do not already have a product of your own. You only have to market and sell the products, you do not have to worry about production, delivery or customer service. You can make a healthy income from affiliate marketing if you have the right audience and choose the right affiliate promotions. In this chapter we will look at how to get started with affiliate marketing. Affiliate marketing is also a great way to promote and sell your own products: read more about this in Chapter 8.

HOW DOES IT WORK?

Affiliate marketing in essence is only slightly more complicated than 'refer a friend' schemes. We have all seen these schemes, you join a gym and they make you an offer whereby if you refer a friend then you get a month's free membership or some high street vouchers or some other incentive. It is basically incentivizing the 'word of mouth' marketing that companies strive for. Word of mouth marketing is more powerful than other types of marketing as the person who recommends the product to you is loyal and trusted, so the marketing message is that bit more authentic.

The idea is that each member refers a friend or preferably a few friends, then the friends refer friends and so on, creating a chain reaction of new sign-ups or purchases. If you have your own products then this is a great way for you to raise the profile of them as well as boost sales. The process of setting up an affiliate program to promote your business is covered in Chapter 8. Read on to find out more about earning through other people's affiliate programmes.

WHY IS AFFILIATE MARKETING SUCH AN ATTRACTIVE WAY TO MAKE MONEY ONLINE?

Affiliate marketing online is a great way to earn an almost passive income; however, do not underestimate the work it initially takes to build the loyalty and trust that are necessary to make sales. Once the hard work is done some internet marketers have likened affiliate marketing to having a 'licence to print money'. Remember, with affiliate marketing you do not have to import, create or deliver the products. You simply make the sale and the money is deposited straight into your bank. What could be easier? Well, hang on a moment and we will tell you why it may not be as easy as all that.

Later in the chapter you can discover exactly how an affiliate marketing promotion works but first let's focus on building this loyal audience that you need to have eating out of the palm of your hand.

CHOOSING YOUR NICHE

The first step to affiliate marketing success is to choose the right niche. You are aiming to build a loyal and trusting audience who are open to being marketed to and who want to buy products and services via you.

When picking a niche you should ...

Consider the competition

An under-serviced market is the best one to aim for. You should look for niches where there is a demand for more information that you can fill. If you can create a blog or newsletter that fills a need, where people can get more information on a particular topic, then this is a very effective way to build an audience and foster the trust and loyalty required to make sales. Do not forget that you do not have to be the one creating the content; you can outsource the content creation by employing ghost writers. This means that, providing you can find an expert to create content, any niche is open to you.

Of course, if you are an expert in a particular field then you may be happy to create the content yourself. You may also choose to enter an established and competitive niche if you already have a level of expertise in that niche as you can create better content than the competition and become the leader in that niche. Chapter 1 will help you make the decision on what niche might be a good one.

Consider the size of the market

Think about the size of the market and how many people you might be able to attract to your email list. Affiliate marketing is very much a numbers game. First you need a market large enough for you to get a sufficient number of people signed up for your email list. Then, you can expect to convert 1–3% sales from that list, although this will vary from niche to niche. This is a conservative estimate based on having 'qualified leads': people who have signed up with the express intention of receiving information on a particular topic. For example, mums of toddlers signing up for a free report on toddler sleep solutions may then be quite keen to purchase various child friendly sleep products.

Consider whether your niche contains people who want to buy

There are lots of people who have a hunger for information in various niches but they are not all buyers and even where they are there are various degrees of money to be made. Niches that are easier to monetize will be ones where the participants earn an above average income or where the hobby or interest requires expensive tools or kit. For example, consider a niche in watercolour painting. Your affiliate promotions could be paintbrushes but unless you have a very large audience it will be difficult to make a lot of money. Obviously you could choose to affiliate market paints, canvasses and a range of other supplies and this would increase your potential earnings. Think now of an alternative niche, photography. The site www.digital-photography-school.com focuses on digital photography and makes money from selling cameras and photography equipment. The price of cameras and equipment is more significant than that of paintbrushes; therefore, you will need to convert fewer sales to make your income target. Another thing to consider is the frequency of purchases required for each niche. You may only buy one camera every two to three years but paint and canvasses? Well, that is a regular purchase for a painter. When considering a niche and which products you will affiliate market you need to consider many factors. Ensure that you have done your homework on the conversion rates, buying patterns and affiliate profit margins of the products you plan to promote before you get started.

Research the affiliate products and services available for promotion

Before you settle on a niche consider what you will affiliate market first. It may be that you spot the products and then build your blog and email list around an interest where you can sell that product. Many top affiliate marketers take this 'back to front' approach. If you have what you think is a viable niche check out what affiliate products there are. Make a list of possible affiliate promotions and what percentage of the sale you would get. Consider how many products you would need to sell to make £2,000 a month, or however much you'd like to earn. Consider the range of products available: you do not want to put all your eggs in one basket. What happens if that one amazing product turns out to be a dud, or the creator/seller pulls it from the market? Be prepared to be flexible with your affiliate promotions.

BUILDING YOUR AUDIENCE

You have chosen your niche and now it is time to build your audience. Do not think this is something that can be done over-night. Give yourself at least six months before you expect to see your first sale. Affiliate marketing is easy work but *only* once the initial hard work has been done. Go back to Chapter 2 where we talked about starting a blog. Get your blog set up and start publishing high quality information on your chosen niche. Focus on your niche as tightly as you can. Do some research into the keywords you wish to target. Do not forget to target 'buying' keywords and phrases, these are the kind of words and phrases people type into a search engine when they want to buy things. For example, the phrase 'make handmade candles' will attract people who want to *make* candles, not *buy* candles. The phrase 'luxury organic candle' is a far better phrase and much more likely to attract those looking to *buy* candles.

Building Your email list

The next step is to attract people to sign up to an email newsletter or email list. You can do this by offering a free product, a discount, more high quality information, a master class: the options here are endless so be creative. Remember that niches can become saturated. Try and set yourself apart from the crowd in as many ways as you can. The reason you want to collate an email list of interested people is that you then have direct access to these people when it comes to doing promotions. Why? Well, according to Mullen & Daniels in *Email Marketing: An Hour a Day*, 'People who are registered to receive email marketing messages from your company will purchase an average of 167% more than those people in your marketing database who are not receiving email.'

Do not forget though that if you constantly sell to your email list without providing any value in between they will likely unsubscribe. A ratio of three value emails to one promotional email should make your subscribers feel that they are being offered the necessary value to stay subscribed. Once you have an established email list you can play around with this ratio, monitor unsubscribes and adjust your ratio accordingly. Read Chapter 3 for more about building a following.

FINDING AFFILIATE MARKETING OPPORTUNITIES

Amazon

Amazon probably has one of the most famous affiliate marketing opportunities known as the 'associates program'. Setting up an account is very quick and simple and Amazon provides you not only with affiliate links but also a range of banners and sidebar search boxes. Amazon works hard for its affiliates as they know that they can increase sales by empowering their affiliates (this is worth noting if you ever decide to launch your own affiliate program). The affiliate rates range from 4–8%; the more sales you make the higher your affiliate percentage band is. This obviously is not a massive percentage rate but it works well for those in niches where the products being sold are a few hundred pounds or more, for example, professional cameras and equipment, mountain bikes etc.

Individual online shops

Such is the power of affiliate marketing to drive sales and build awareness that many individual online shops now have an affiliate marketing program. You can find most affiliate programs by scrolling to the foot of the company's homepage where there is usually a link.

Affiliate Future

Affiliate Future, an affiliate marketing network, is like a warehouse where you will find affiliate programs from a huge variety of companies suitable for all niches. Percentages paid on the sales you make vary widely so check out all your options before settling on certain programmes (or a single network).

Other affiliate marketing networks include:

- Affiliate Bot (www.affiliatebot.com)
- Affiliate Window (www.affiliatewindow.com)
- CPA Way (www.cpaway.com)
- Paid on Results (www.paidonresults.com)
- The Slice (www.theslice.co.uk)
- Trade Doubler (www.tradedoubler.com)

Clickbank

Clickbank is a very popular marketplace for information products. You can both sell your own products and promote other people's products on the site. Founded in 1998 Clickbank is considered a market leader for information products, with 50,000 products and 100,000 affiliate marketers. As an affiliate marketer you can simply set up an account and peruse the vast array of products, picking the ones most suitable to your niche. You can then lift code for banners and text links and Clickbank will track any sales you make. Payments are made automatically via Clickbank.

Commission Junction

Commission Junction offers similar services to Clickbank. It is helpful to have accounts with a few different sites as this will extend the range of products from which you can choose. Commission Junction focuses a lot of energy on optimizing pay for performance marketing. To promote high performance they publish performance metrics of advertisers, publishers and ads. This is helpful for an affiliate marketer as if you are a high performing marketer, publishers will seek you out to forge exclusive partnerships with better revenue sharing deals.

E-junkie

E-junkie is a shopping cart provider that allows you to use 'buy now' buttons to sell your own goods and services via your website. E-junkie also acts as a marketplace in its own right as well as having easy to manage affiliate programmes that help you extend your reach and drive sales. E-junkie will track your sales and provide a report to the publisher who will then make the affiliate payments. The site explains, 'You can sell ebooks, sell mp3 tracks and albums, sell software, icons, fonts, artwork, phone cards, event tickets, cds, posters, books, t-shirts and almost everything else you want to sell.'

Affiliate opportunities in your personal network

Some of the most lucrative affiliate opportunities are for internet-based information products, such as eBooks, training programmes and membership sites. Percentages can be as high as 50% or more as the product has low costs for the provider to create. Look to your network and see who is creating their own products: the likelihood is that they have an affiliate program for you to join.

If your network is not established yet, try Clickbank and E-junkie where you will find information products suitable for all niches. Again, referral percentages vary so do some thorough research. You may also want to purchase the product and try it out yourself first. The worst thing that can happen to an affiliate marketer is to promote a substandard product to their audience as this can break the trust and loyalty that is so difficult to build up.

DOING AN AFFILIATE PROMOTION

Finally, once you have built an audience and provided them with lots of free value it is time to do your first affiliate marketing promotion. You have come this far so you didn't think it was just going to be a case of sticking a link up and crossing your fingers, did you? No, marketing is a slightly more intricate process than that. To effectively market the product you need to follow the AIDA strategy, which was developed over a hundred years ago by an American sales pioneer, E. St Elmo Lewis, and which stands for Attention, Interest, Desire and Action.

Attention

The first step of the affiliate promotion should gain the reader's attention and make them aware of the product you are promoting. Note that no 'hard' selling should take place at this stage. A blog post and email newsletter highlighting the product is all that's required. This may take place well before the launch of a product in a 'look what is about to launch' type approach.

Interest

The second stage is creating interest in the product. In a blog post and email newsletter it is up to you to describe what is interesting about the product, what its unique features are, what it does etc. ...

Desire

The third stage is creating desire and this is done through selling the benefits of the product. What is the benefit to your reader of purchasing the product, why should they purchase this product over the alternatives?

Action

The final stage is getting the reader to take action, which in this case is purchasing the product. This is where the hard sell comes in and where you may highlight the time limit on buying or any scarcity there is, for example, if the product is about to run out.

Case study: Pat Flynn of Smart Passive Income

www.smartpassiveincome.com

Pat Flynn writes about internet business and making a passive income online. When he was made redundant from his architect's position in 2008 he turned to the internet to replace his income.

Three years on, Pat has broken through the barrier to earn over $30,000 in a month. He says, 'I still can't believe it, it's amazing'.

Pat works for around four hours a day on various online projects and spends the rest of his time with his wife and young son. For Pat the 'internet lifestyle' affords him the ultimate luxury, 'It's not about an internet lifestyle travelling around the world for me, I'm happy at home doing normal stuff and having time to focus on the thing that matters to me, my family'.

Pat's first success came when he created a training resource for an architecture exam. He had a unique insight into the studying required to pass the exam as he'd not long taken it himself. He leveraged his knowledge and this product alone has netted him thousands of dollars. Pat embarked on some internet marketing training of his own and implemented what he learned by adding an audio recording to the training package. Pat says, 'I pretty much doubled the income from that product overnight by simply adding the audio'. Looking for further ways to improve his offering he approached a company that sold practice exams and asked if they had an affiliate marketing scheme. Pat says, 'I knew this company had a great offering that I couldn't improve upon, and didn't want to compete with. Promoting their stuff and getting a cut of the profits is easy as it's a great product that people who buy my resource really need. Plus I don't have to worry about stock, delivery or customer service. It's win win'.

Pat promotes a range of products including hosting and software such as Market Samurai. His affiliate commissions now account for half of all his earnings, over $15,000 a month. He promotes a number of different products and services but only those that he's used and finds value in:

> I have two rules when it comes to affiliate marketing. Firstly I must have used it myself, and secondly it needs to be good. My readers trust me and I don't want to jeopardise

that. Not for any product and certainly not to make a quick buck. I also don't believe in hard selling to people, if they want it they'll buy it.

Pat's interests now range from blogs, eBooks and training programmes through to affiliate marketing and even iPhone Apps. He has no plans to return to full-time employment and is looking at other ways to build his brand online.

TAKE ACTION

Are you ready to do your first affiliate marketing promotion? Do some research into the affiliate products that may appeal to your audience. Try out the product if you can. Once you're satisfied that the product is good quality and represents good value, create an affiliate promotion campaign that encompasses the AIDA model.

8 Affiliate Marketing Your Products

In the last chapter we covered affiliate marketing as a way to earn passive income from your blog, your email list and your social media following.

Now we are flipping it over. If you have created products of your own such as eBooks and eCourses then you will want to start recruiting people to help you market and sell these products. Even if you sell tangible products like candles or t-shirts, setting up an affiliate scheme is a great way to raise the profile of your brand and make more sales. In short you need to build your own army of affiliates to make the job of finding new buyers easier.

Your net only spreads so far and once you have sold to all the interested parties in your circle of reach, then what? Well this is where your affiliates come into play. You can basically leverage their audience to reach a whole new market of potential buyers. Many of your connections will be interested in becoming affiliates as it can be a good way to make money when you do not have a product of your own. If you haven't already got a product to sell refer to Chapters 4 and 6 for inspiration.

AFFILIATE MARKETING BASICS

At its core, affiliate marketing is all about relationships. The success of an affiliate marketing campaign relies on your relationship with your affiliates and your affiliates' relationship with their audience. As with any relationship it is important to build and maintain respect and trust. Respect your affiliates by ensuring that you keep them well informed and pay them on time. They are trying to make a living too! If you do these two things then your affiliates will grow to trust you and will want to work with you on future product launches and promotions.

Your affiliates are a font of knowledge in your niche. As a product provider you may even liaise with them on what products and services *they* think the buyers want. You can also gain other information like good times to launch. Always communicate with your affiliates well before a launch; launches take time and you want to make sure that your affiliates mark yours in their diary.

CREATING AN AFFILIATE PROGRAM

There are a few ways to set up an affiliate program, from basic through to complex. For information products that can be digitally delivered one of the easiest options is to sign up to a site like Clickbank or E-junkie. These sites allow you to sell your products but they also have very efficient affiliate programmes built in where sales are tracked and you simply pay the fees by PayPal.

If you are selling tangible and/or information products you can also set up your own affiliate programme through 1ShoppingCart and some other cart providers. A tech person can add various features to these affiliate programmes to customize them for your needs. You can also have an entire customized system created for you but there is a cost attached to this.

Affiliate resources

The first thing you need to do is consider what resources your partners will need to effectively promote your product. The more you provide your affiliates with stimulus for promoting your products the more likely they are to do so. It is important to make everything as accessible as you can. Not everyone will be technically able. Read on to find out what resources you should provide and how you can help your less tech savvy affiliates.

Text links

The most basic promotional tool is a text link. This is a link that can be embedded into promotional copy that will track sales. Your affiliates can write a review of your product and they can embed this link within the review in various places. Provide your affiliate partner with the code for the link and tell them how the anchor text can be changed to reflect any call to action the affiliate wants.

Banner ads

Affiliates like to see a variety of banners in all shapes and sizes. You need to consider the variety of websites that may choose to promote your products and ensure that you offer something to suit all header and sidebar spaces. You may want to offer animated options too. Consider the colours, images and text that will most likely grab the attention of your target market.

Banners are not really effective on their own as they lack a clear call to action and some blog readers can become blind to them. For best effect use them as awareness raisers alongside direct calls to action such as emails and blog posts. Rotate and change the banners often so that the reader notices them more often.

Email copy

For those affiliates with newsletters, pre-written email copy is very handy as it saves on the affiliate's time. By providing email templates you can also have a big hand in what is said about your product and how it is promoted. Take a short course or read a book on marketing and/or copywriting to sell: try *Persuasive Writing* by Peter Frederick.

Good affiliate marketers will be busy working on a range of projects. It is your job to make it as easy as possible for them to promote your products and make sales. They may not have time to read books on marketing and copywriting; arm yourself with the knowledge and send them an eLesson or tip sheet with the main points bulleted. Help them to help you!

If you can, provide your affiliates with a number of emails for various stages of your campaign. You can employ the AIDA (Attention, Interest, Desire, Action) model from Chapter 7 to ensure maximum conversion. Encourage your affiliates to edit these template emails to suit their own audiences. It is important that the audience 'hears' the voice of the affiliate, not you.

Blog copy

As with the emails, create some template blog posts that your affiliates can pick up and edit to suit their needs. Copying and editing a pre-written blog post loaded with all the facts and necessary information is a much quicker and more desirable job than having to research everything and then write a lengthy blog post. You do not want there to be any barriers stopping your affiliates from promoting your product so try and put yourself in their shoes. Think what would make it easier for you as an affiliate to promote and make sales. Make a list and work through each of the barriers making it easier and easier and you will see an increase in promotional activity amongst your affiliates.

Video

Promoting and selling via video is the most cutting edge way to affiliate market products at the moment. Why not create some face-to-camera videos about your products that affiliates can embed alongside a call to action. Or go a step further and encourage affiliates to create their own videos about your products. Do not forget that some affiliates may not know how to shoot and upload video so perhaps a little tutorial would be helpful.

Be as creative as you can in your videos to grab maximum attention.

Recruiting affiliates

Once your affiliate program is set up and you have loaded your resource area with banners, links, emails, blog posts and videos it is time to start recruiting your affiliates. Think carefully about your ideal affiliate. Think of people who have large audiences or email lists, market leaders who have a strong voice and a lot of trust and loyalty. These are the type of people who will best be able to sell your products and services. Send them an email inviting them to join.

Unless you vet applicants, once you open the doors to your affiliate programme you do not really have any control over who will join. Bear in mind that many of the people who join will not necessarily have a full understanding of affiliate marketing or how to sell so schedule in some time to consider how you can help improve your affiliates' understanding of what is required and show them how they can get the best from your program.

There are a number of ways you can recruit affiliates:

Blog posts

You can start spreading the message about your new affiliate program by writing a blog post about it. Do not assume that people will know what affiliate marketing is though so start by explaining what it is. Then you can go on and sell the benefits and say who it is most ideal for, i.e. people with targeted audiences, large email newsletter lists etc.

Social media

Put the word out about your affiliate program across your social media sites and encourage your contacts to pass the message on. You need to try and reach as many people as possible to find the most ideal affiliates.

Email your lists

If you have email lists or a newsletter do an article highlighting your new affiliate program and how it works. Encourage people to join up and just give it a go. From your point of view the more people promoting your products the better, whether they sell or no, as it builds brand awareness and can encourage people to buy later on too.

Ask your customers

Some of the best people to promote your products are the ones who know and love them. These people will find it very easy to sell the benefits of your products and are most likely to convince their audience through their natural passion for what you do. Ask your customers if they have blogs or websites and see if they'd be interested in becoming an affiliate. If you have a few 'raving fans' contact them directly.

Approach influential people in your niche

Figure out who the big players are in your niche. Who has a big audience or a large email list? Remember, affiliate marketing is partially about numbers. If you know that you convert 1% of people when they hit your sales page then you can work out how many people you need to drive there to make X amount of sales. When approaching 'big players', contact these people personally and explain what you are doing. Explain how you can work in a mutually beneficial partnership. Be ready to answer questions and negotiate terms with them.

Links on your website

Promote your program by adding an affiliate page to your site, and banners or links in its sidebar or footer.

Affiliates referring affiliates

Going a step further you can even encourage your affiliates to refer other affiliates. You can offer a percentage of the affiliate's sales or a one-off payment as an incentive.

Help your affiliates sell

Help your affiliates sell by providing marketing advice in the form of emails. It might even be a good idea to create a video tutorial on how to navigate your affiliate resource area and how to do things like place banners on their sites. You can film tutorials like this using Jing or Camtasia. If you really want to go the extra mile you could hold a webinar for your affiliates where you can teach them exactly what to do and also answer any questions they have. Removing the obstacles to your affiliates promoting is key to your success.

Encourage your affiliates to promote

Keep your products and promotional campaign at the forefront of your affiliate partners' minds by sending them short but regular emails. During a promotion or campaign keep your affiliates up to date about how sales are going. Timely reminders of how much money everyone is making can be a real incentive for affiliates to raise their promotional efforts.

Some top marketers like to add additional incentives in the form of leader boards and prizes for top affiliates. Consider whether this is something that would work in your niche. Some people may thrive on this kind of competitive approach to marketing; others will find it intimidating and off-putting. Ask your affiliates if they would welcome such a scheme. In the information marketing niche popular prizes include widescreen TVs, iPads and web design vouchers. Think about your niche and what would make relevant and appropriate prizes. For example, if your affiliates are women a treat worth winning might be a spa day.

Choose senior partners

Having senior affiliate partners is important as these are the people who will raise awareness of your brand and are most likely to drive the most sales. Make a list of the top five people in your niche you would most like to have associated with your product. Contact these people personally and explain what you are doing and what the benefits are to them being involved.

For these senior partners it is both necessary and worthwhile to go the extra mile in terms of customizing your offer for them. Options include creating dedicated co-branded pages; this works really well if you are working with an already established network. Having the co-branding – for example, a picture and quote from the leader of that network – can help you build trust and credibility with the audience, which will lead to increased sales. You could also do dedicated webinars, additional bonuses and/or special offers. The scope here is endless so be imaginative and think about what will work for that particular segment.

Be committed to the relationship with your senior partners; keep them updated on payment schedules and send thank you letters following a campaign. Once things have died down from the launch think of other ways in which you can promote each other and work together in the future.

TAKE ACTION

If you already have products to sell then start thinking about how you can use affiliate marketing to help you raise sales, extend your reach and build your business right now. Have a look at some of the services we have mentioned and think about which service would work best for your business. Do some costings, work out what you can afford to pay affiliates and start by setting up a simple programme. You can get more complex later on.

9 Monetizing Your Blog

Once you have built up a nice stream of traffic then you may feel it is time for your blog to start paying its way. You can read about Yaro Starak in Chapter 4: he was able to start making $1,000 with just 300 visitors a day so check your blog stats and see how close you are to being ready to host your first few advertisements. There are lots of ways to monetize your blog and we will cover most of them in this chapter. Many bloggers won't focus on just one income stream for their blog. Testing each monetization method to see how it converts in your niche and then settling on the top three is a good strategy.

Case Study: Asha Dornfest – from mum blogging to earning a full-time income

www.parenthacks.com

When Asha started blogging about parenting in 2005 it was never her intention for it to become her job: 'the idea of making money from blogging was about as far-fetched as making money from talking to my friends on the phone'. Asha quickly realized that what she loved about blogging were the practical and community elements and so she launched Parent Hacks in December 2005. Parent Hacks is a community site where practical parenting tips and 'hacks' are shared and visitors can become both readers and contributors.

The site grew quickly. Asha says,

> At the time, there were no other parenting sites that used a
> blog as the backbone of a community conversation – most
> blogs were personal journals. So Parent Hacks naturally
> appealed to a wider audience. Also, the focus on practicality
> and problem-solving was something different in online parent-
> ing 'media' at the time. This take on parenting appealed to
> both moms and dads, and cut across a number of other audi-
> ences: tech/geek, green/environmental, crafty, and those
> interested in personal productivity, food, travel, and DIY.

About a year after launching Parent Hacks, Asha started monetizing the site:

> I contacted Federated Media in February of 2006. Parent
> Hacks had gotten good exposure right out of the gate
> mostly due to links from Boing Boing and Blogging Baby
> (now AOL's ParentDish). FM was a startup with only one
> other member of its parenting federation – Dooce, who had
> kicked off the parenting blog phenomenon with her distinc-
> tive voice. Parent Hacks was nowhere near Dooce in terms
> of size, influence or style, but FM saw its potential and asked
> me to join. John Batelle's vision and the other early employ-
> ees' tireless work were incredibly inspiring, and helped me
> realize that Parent Hacks could serve a dual purpose as my
> community forum and a business. I also included Amazon
> Associates links in Parent Hacks content when they made
> sense, and have from the beginning.

Asha says the most successful monetization methods have been
the Amazon Associates program (covered in Chapter 7, Selling
Other People's Products), banner ads and dedicated campaigns
arranged by Federated Media. She also does freelance work as a

result of Parent Hacks. Asha gives this advice for those aiming to monetize their blog or niche website. 'Focus on the content and the community, and build a truly useful site your readers can trust. The only way to create a lasting, meaningful site (or brand, if you want to think about it in those terms) is to provide your readers with something they need and can feel good about supporting and recommending.'

WHEN SHOULD I MONETIZE?

Two questions that always come up when discussing how to monetize a blog or website are 'when's the right time?' and 'how much traffic do I need?' Yaro says, 'You can start trying to monetise your blog from the beginning but whether you will make any money or whether companies will want to advertise is another thing.'

The bloggers that we have interviewed in this book spent between six months and a year working on their blogs and building their audience before they began any sort of monetization, so this should give you a rough guide as to when is a good time to start. Professional blogger Natalie Lue says, 'Although traffic is important it is about having a unique selling proposition too and seeing yourself as a brand, once you get to around 8–10,000 unique users a month you can charge a decent rate.' In terms of traffic you may be able to start making your first few pounds from a hundred visitors a day. Then you can raise your prices as your traffic increases.

HOW SHOULD I MONETIZE?

A good place to start is with a rates page on your blog/website. Here you can break down your prices, or advertise set packages. You may wish to write about the demographics of your audience and give some traffic statistics. If you want to automate the process of selling banners on your site you can get PayPal buttons that allow advertisers to 'buy now'.

How can I find advertisers?

When you first start out taking advertising on your blog it probably won't be the case that advertisers are queuing up at your door to place ads with you (if it is, then lucky you!). You are probably going to have to go out and find your first few advertisers to get the ball rolling. Look at your niche and think about the companies that you think may be interested in advertising with you. Contact these companies and offer them an introductory rate for a few months. Now look at the other blogs and websites in your niche. Which companies are already paying for blog ads? These companies obviously see the value in this type of advertising so they can be considered 'warm' leads and you should definitely approach them with an introductory rate.

Spotting advertising opportunities

As you become a more high profile blogger you will start to find that you are approached a lot to review products and print press releases etc. Every time someone contacts you with such a request it is an opportunity for you to sell advertising. The person or company has already identified you as someone they'd like to work with and who would be a great match for their product or service so all you have to do is make a counter offer.

How much should I charge?

This is a 'how long's a piece of string?' question as really you should charge as much as the advertisers are willing to pay but of course that's difficult to find out. Start with checking out your competitors' pricing, especially those who are clearly selling ads as they are likely to have some realistic figures. Now look at the cost of comparative advertising on Facebook, Google Adwords, papers, magazine ads etc.

Consider how much ad space you have and how much you'd like to earn. You will probably want to sell some ad spots at a premium and some at a bit less. For example, ads 'above the fold' (the bit you see before you have to scroll) are far more valuable to an advertiser than an ad further down the page. Think about the range of advertising you might offer and how the value differs.

Take all the information you collate and come up with some rough figures for your various advertisement options. Start your prices off at the lower end of your scale and aim to book yourself out. Advertisers will be keener to advertise on a site that is sold out or has limited space as this gives the perception that other advertisers are finding value there.

Once you are sold out you can increase your prices gradually and the key is to manage supply and demand by keeping your prices just at the right level to ensure that you are always *almost* booked out. Do not be tempted to make drastic price increases, as with every business there are quieter and busier times so give it a few months before deciding to put prices up. It is much better to have to make small price increases often than to have to put prices down. Putting prices down sends the message that advertisers are leaving as they are not finding value.

MONETIZATION STRATEGIES

AdSense

The AdSense program is run by Google and is probably the most well-known way of making money amongst bloggers. You basically sign up and add some code to your blog's template. The code serves textual advertising to your blog; each time one of those ads is clicked you make money, usually a few pence. AdSense used to be extremely common and popular until other ways of making money were created. AdSense is very easy to use; however, it is very difficult to make a substantial amount of money unless you have a blog that receives a lot of page views. If your site incorporates a forum then give it a go as forums generate a high volume of page views. It is worth noting that there is a general feeling that AdSense can be a bit unsightly and therefore off-putting to readers, but you will need to make your own mind up about that.

Reviews/advertorials

In the blogosphere these are often called 'blog features' or 'sponsored posts'. They basically involve you writing a post on behalf of the client. This may take the form of a review, advertorial or competition. You would usually charge 'per post' for these. Sponsored posts are easy to do and you do not need a ton of traffic to deliver reasonable value. If you are clever with how the post is written you can also create a piece of high quality content in the process. It may be that some clients won't be aware that this is a service you offer so you can add this as an option on your advertise page or you can make the suggestion when a PR sends you a press release or asks you to promote something.

Be aware though that too many sponsored posts can spoil your blog and that sponsored posts in any form can be off-putting to readers. Depending on the post it can also take a bit of time to do the appropriate research and then the time to write the post. They are a good option for blogs with a targeted audience as if you make the right match in terms of product or service the post could be highly interesting to your readership. Sponsored posts can turn into a good earner if you can book them regularly enough. Just one sponsored post a week at a rate of £125 per post is £6,500 every year.

Selling text links

Before we get into the nuts and bolts of selling text links: a word of warning. It is somewhat controversial and some search engines do not really like the practice of people buying and selling text links as it is seen as trying to rig the system. Nevertheless, it does happen and there is a market for it.

Selling links involves you posting a hypertext link either in your sidebar or in the main content of your site. The client will usually have set anchor text they want you to use. This will tie in with the keywords they are targeting. You would usually sell these links in blocks of months, e.g. £100 for three months. If you want to sell these automatically you can do so by setting up a page where clients can purchase and install the PayPal 'buy now' buttons. Make sure you have terms and conditions stating that you can refuse text ads, or indeed any type of advertising, with content that is unsuitable for your site.

Text links are very easy to place and they do not take up much space at all so you can sell quite a few without your blog looking crowded. On a negative note, text links can look a little unsightly in the sidebar. Traffic is less important for selling text links but many advertisers will look for a good page rank. You can check your page rank by searching for 'check page rank' in Google.

Post sponsor

This is where a client sponsors one of your posts. Basically you put a sentence with a link at the foot of one of your posts. For example: 'This post is sponsored by Angel Stationery (link), unique stationery for special occasions'. The demand for this form of advertising is lower than other types; however, it suits some types of advertisers who want links in the main content section of your blog. The advantage to the publisher is that it is a discreet form of advertising as it does not force a break in the blogger's own content. It is also very easy to add a sentence and link at the foot of the post. The demand for this has diminished over the years; advertisers seem to prefer paying a premium for a post of their own now. However, it is worth offering a variety of advertising options for all budgets and this can be at the lower end of the price scale.

Banner ads

There are two types of banner ad: banners that you host and sell yourself and banners that are served to you via an intermediary. We are going to cover the former first and the latter will be covered later on in this chapter. For privately hosted banner ads the client should provide you with the code that you then paste into your sidebar. It is very simple to update and change ads if you have a widgetized sidebar, which is the norm for most WordPress blogs, by using a plug-in like Kadom Ads.

You can charge by the month or for longer periods. Most advertisers will want the ad as high up the page as possible, maybe even 'above the fold' where you can see it without scrolling down the page. Remember, the closer to the top of the page the more you can charge. Many publishers like selling their own banner ads as they can be choosy over who they sell to and they can negotiate on price. Charging for placement rather than per click is nearly always more lucrative for small to medium blogs. A downside to banners is that they take up quite a bit of sidebar space and to the reader they are very obviously advertising, which can be off-putting.

Advertising intermediaries

Glam, Handpicked Media and Federated Media are all examples of advertising intermediaries. They aim to bring publishers and advertisers together. When you sign up for an account with one of these companies they give you code to paste into the template of your blog and the ads are then served to you automatically. This makes it a very passive form of income but you make a little less, of course, as the intermediaries take a percentage of the fee. You are usually paid for impressions: that is a certain amount of money for each time the banner is loaded. Therefore, it is the number of page views that really counts if you are trying to make money from this form of advertising. The advantage is that it is easy to set up an account and then you do not have to worry about finding or managing clients. So if selling and negotiating is not your thing then this could be a good alternative.

Affiliate Future

Affiliate Future (along with the other networks listed on page 127) allows you to promote products and businesses using text links and banners (which they provide) and you are paid a commission on any sales you make. Each company you can promote has a different set of rules on how commission can be earned so check them out individually. Affiliate Future and its competitors are easy to join and you do not need to deal with clients directly. You do have to make sales to earn money though and the banners require space in your sidebar. Affiliate marketing like this is great if you are in a specific niche, especially if that niche is product related.

Selling branded products

Sites like Cafepress and Zazzle allow you to brand your own apparel and products such as mugs and keyrings with a logo or tagline etc. You can then sell these via your Cafepress shop, which you can advertise on your blog, usually in the sidebar. These sites focus on usability so it is easy to set up an account and begin designing. You will need a very dedicated (and fairly large) following if you are to make money.

Clickbank and Commission Junction

Clickbank and Commission Junction are marketplaces for information products, predominantly eBooks. You can sign up as an affiliate and promote your chosen products. You will receive commission on sales. Commission varies product to product and there are products on thousands of topics so it is easy to find several suitable ones in your niche. It is easy to join these sites and one of the advantages is that no product handling is required.

Amazon Associates program

This is an affiliate program where you can promote Amazon products by embedding links into your posts. If someone buys something via your link you earn a commission, usually between 4–8%. It is simple to get started and the links are fairly unobtrusive on your blog. The Amazon Associates program is perfect for blogs with an audience that likes to buy.

Blog sponsor

This involves one company sponsoring your entire blog. This may involve banner ads, blog features and perhaps some theming too. The advantage of this is that you do not need to seek out further sponsors and your income is guaranteed. The negatives are that your income is fixed and you are tied to the company.

Case Study: Natalie Lue, professional blogger

www.natalielue.co.uk

Natalie started blogging in June 2004 after going on a bad date. She started off recounting her experiences with men along with her life experiences, 'I was giving people snapshots of my life...it was fun'. She'd considered niche websites but didn't consider making money from blogging until a bit later on. By 2006 Natalie was getting 10,000 readers a month on her blog Baggage Reclaim and was featured in the *Daily Express*.

Before becoming a professional blogger in January 2008 Natalie was an IT publisher. During her maternity leave she launched her second site Bambino Goodies which grew to 4,000 readers a month and at that point she left her job and focused on monetizing her sites and doing some consultancy work. After hosting advertising across both sites she decided to write her first self-help eBook based on relationships, which was published in February 2008. She sold this for £7 via her newsletter.

Bambino Goodies grew rapidly during 2008 and Natalie monetized this site predominantly with banner advertising, which she booked and negotiated herself, 'I was approached by intermediary companies but I had a firm idea of the type of advertising I wanted to host and I didn't want any conflicting message, plus they take a big cut of the fee.' The site now generates five figures a year in advertising revenue.

Natalie went on to release further eBooks on her Baggage Reclaim site, which continues to be a source of income for her: 'Although one of my sites is predominantly monetised by advertising I do believe in diversification so eBooks, consultancy and having other streams of income is really important to me.' In total Natalie's company is on target to earn over six figures in 2011. Natalie still believes there are plenty of opportunities online to make an income, 'Put in the graft and you will make an income, it won't be immediate and you will have to put some effort in but it is possible.'

CONTRACTS

Once you start to take money for advertising you are, in effect, setting up a contract with the business paying for the advert. It is advisable to get terms and conditions for your site, which advertisers have to agree to. This makes it clear what you are offering and can give you some protection in case of disagreements.

TAKE ACTION

Ready to start monetizing your blog? Decide what type of advertising you want to offer, make space in sidebars and headers and have clear places to offer banner ads. You want to catch the advertiser's eye and show them that by advertising in that spot they too could catch the eye of their target audience.

• Think about your ideal advertisers and what type of advertising might convert best

• Check out other blogs and websites in your niche and see which companies are advertising on them

• Create an 'advertise' page with details about what you offer in terms of ad options, packages and prices

• Start contacting the companies you have identified who you think may be potentially interested in advertising on your blog

10 Make Money Online from Writing

I f you can write, you are on your way to making a living online. There is a continual need for good content, and a wide variety of outlets to write for. It can be a competitive field: as well as people who start earning a living from writing online, more and more print journalists are seeing an increasing proportion of their income coming from creating web content.

The key to earning a good living from online writing is negotiating a good deal for yourself and picking off the more lucrative jobs: the competitive nature of this field can mean that there are many low-paid opportunities. Do not just consider straight copywriting: if you are adept with Twitter and Facebook you can gain work as a social media consultant, which can be better paid. If you have expertise in a specific niche, look for writing work in this area to command better rates.

If you have vision and planning skills, you can move on to contracting other writers to work for you, which can help you grow your income in a way that you can't if you simply exchange time for money as a writer. Read on to discover the essential knowledge you need to make money online by writing, and the pitfalls to avoid.

DEMAND AND OPPORTUNITIES

If you have followed advice in earlier chapters of this book and started your own blog, you will know that there is a constant need for good content. As well as satisfying followers, search engines will rank a site more highly if it is updated on a regular basis. Here are twelve ideas for online writing work:

- Writing marketing emails
- Creating SMS marketing campaigns
- Devising pay per click campaigns
- Ghost blogging for businesses
- Writing sponsored posts for your own blogs
- Creating articles for businesses
- Writing eNewsletter content
- Creating website editorial content
- Reviewing products
- Setting up Facebook pages
- Creating Twitter campaigns
- Writing eBooks for others

Social networking is an area of growing demand for online work. It is a fast growing area where practical and demonstrable experience can beat the need for formal qualifications. More and more businesses can see the need to reach out via social media but some have already experienced the backlash of doing so in an uninformed manner, while others do not know where to start. If you can create campaigns to raise awareness virally using Twitter and Facebook, and via interactions with bloggers, you can find yourself in demand. If you have good blogging skills, you can offer freelance support to companies who do not have the expertise or time to blog.

If you have an area of specialist expertise you can create your own well-paid niche where you can provide expert content.

SPECIALIST WRITING SKILLS FOR THE WEB

Writing for the web is a different skill to writing for print media, and you will need to be aware of the different approach required. Here are some tips to help you:

Length

Some people find it harder to scan a page online than in print. Therefore, web pages tend to be shorter, around 200–300 words in length. Keep your copy clear and focused on the point. If you have lots to get in, break it into multiple pages or posts. Avoid long paragraphs and use shorter words rather than longer ones to ensure maximum readability, whatever the reader's educational level. Consider how much of your content will be above the fold: that can offer a guideline as to how much you should write for maximum effect. Remember that text will be viewed at different resolutions on different size screens.

Structure

Maximize the use of bullet points, short sections and navigational links to other pages to make it easy for readers to scan and find their way. For anyone with a research background, online content creation should be a joy. You should make a positive feature of linking back to sites or articles that you refer to, not just in academia but in the blogosphere and indeed from any website.

Ensure that you understand the keywords that the site owner is focusing on for SEO. Incorporate these words and phrases in a natural way without overusing them. Always prioritize text that makes sense to a human reader over that which might attract a search engine!

Add structure and aid navigation with the use of headlines and anchored subheads too. These should also reflect the key phrases if you are writing for SEO, and should be mirrored in the tags.

Interactivity

Web content is different to most print content in that readers expect to be able to interact. Within your copy can they contact you, follow a link for more depth, be persuaded by a call to action, register, become interested in an advertiser or sponsor link or buy a product? When you next browse the web just look at the many different ways you move from page to page and site to site.

Finally, you need to be able to review your own work and pick up errors in grammar, spelling and consistency. In the fast moving world of online publishing many companies operate without professional editors or proofreaders and so accurate delivery of copy is vital. Do not rely on a spell checker: do get a good dictionary. Practise scanning for errors by reading text aloud or even reviewing it from back to front as this makes your brain view familiar words in a new way, so you are more likely to detect errors.

WHAT EVERY WRITER NEEDS TO KNOW

Whatever sort of content you are creating there are a few legal basics that every writer should know. If you write something, the copyright is yours unless you sign a contract assigning it to the publisher. Be aware that you need to be able to back up everything that you write with facts and research: get a basic understanding of the laws on libel, contempt of court, privacy and breach of confidence. Find out about the Data Protection Act and Freedom of Information Act too if you are in the UK at www.ico.gov.uk.

Beyond what you need to know, it is also helpful if you are able to use recording equipment. Firstly, you may want to interview people and write up the conversation, and secondly publishers may now want video and audio reports as well as written content. More and more phones have excellent quality recording equipment. Practise with yours, and acquire an external microphone as this can improve sound quality in a face-to-face interview. Look at ways to record conference calls on the telephone and, for a few dollars, download the Pamela software to allow you to record Skype (VoIP) calls.

Finally, if writing looks like becoming a significant part of your income, consider joining the National Union of Journalists. It is open to staff and freelancers, editors, photographers and public relations professionals, as well as journalists. It can advise you on freelance fees, contracts, copyright, and will help you if clients are not paying up on time. See www.nuj.org.uk for full details. The Society of Authors is also helpful if you write books.

Read more about earning through writing in *Commercial Writing – How to Earn a Living as a Business Writer* by Antonia Chitty.

WHERE'S THE MONEY?

Web writing can be poorly paid. It can take time to find more profitable clients, and the more popular you are the easier it is to only take on well-paying jobs. Focus on spreading the word about your high quality work and the unique aspects of your services to boost your profile and the amount people will pay. Testimonials from customers help boost your perceived value so ask for these every time you complete work and display them prominently on the site.

Social networking sites like LinkedIn, Ecademy, Twitter and even Facebook can help you find work, stay in touch with former colleagues and clients and promote your business. The work you have been doing from Chapter 3 to build your profile as an expert will ensure that people are aware of you and your writing expertise. Make it clear via social media what services you can offer and draw people in to a page on your site or blog where you lay this out in more detail.

Proof of your writing skills is vital to finding new work. If you have no other work to showcase, start blogging today (see Chapter 2). Many people earning a living online have started by blogging, which is why we recommend it so early on in this book. Once you have some writing on your own site, you may need to offer to write for others at no cost to develop your portfolio. Update your site every time you write a new article and tweet about new content. Include plenty of relevant keywords to help people discover you via search engines. Link to other sites that you have written for, and include testimonials with links back to the client's website.

Get clear about the clients you want to target, and how you will reach them. If you are clear about your target audience and the media they consume your promotion efforts will work better. Targeting local businesses? Use local networks to reach them. Looking to get involved with digital and new media companies? Approach them by email or link up on Twitter in the first instance, and have your CV available electronically.

In *Commercial Writing – How to Earn a Living as a Business Writer*, I advise:

> If you are thinking of pitching to a magazine site, read the site, find out about submission guidelines, and make sure you have some examples of other things you have written in the same sphere. Similarly, if you are approaching businesses to offer your services in improving their website content, or as a paid blogger, have relevant examples of similar work. Ideally, you should also be able to show the results you have achieved with other websites, and concrete details of the increased numbers of visitors to the client's site as a result.

Look online for freelance writing directories and journalism job sites: there are plenty of them and some are listed in *Commercial Writing – How to Earn a Living as a Business Writer*. Remember, though, that sites like Elance and PeoplePerHour are open to anyone and the sheer number of people competing for work across the globe can drive the price you are paid right down. You will find better-paid work by networking in real life via business or media networking events and by joining online forums and email groups.

In order to get many journalism jobs, for on- or offline writing, you need to be able to pitch. A pitch is a short paragraph that you send to a commissioning editor outlining your idea for an article and why you are ideally placed to write it. Study the publication, sum up your idea in 100–200 words, and follow up with a call. Persistence and tenacity may be required to succeed in what can be a competitive area.

Negotiating payment

Some jobs will be advertised with a fixed rate that you will probably have to settle for. If, over time, you make yourself indispensable to a publication and find you are writing for them on a regular basis you can begin to negotiate your rate.

With other writing work you will be asked for a quote. Look at the NUJ's 'Rate for the Job' website http://www.londonfreelance. org/feesguide/index.php?section=Welcome, which outlines what other freelancers have earned for work in a range of sectors.

Rates of pay for online writing can be low: some sites seem very much aimed at the enthusiastic amateur who has another source of income, people willing to work at below minimum wage, those living in countries with a relatively low cost of living or the person who can create articles in bulk. Blog networks in the UK can pay from a few pounds per post upwards, depending on the size and stature of the business and what they feel they can get away with.

WHERE TO WRITE AND WHAT THE DEAL IS

There are a number of web information providers such as Bukisa, Suite 101 and About.com that take on writers. You get paid depending on the revenue generated from advertisements on your pages. There can be extensive interview processes for this sort of position where you have to create significant amounts of content with no guarantee of income.

Bukisa

Upload articles and earn a share of the revenue from your content by embedding your own Google AdSense code within your publications. You can reprint articles you have published elsewhere, but Bukisa advise that original articles perform better. Be aware that you will need a large back catalogue of articles on Bukisa before you'll make any real income. If you have lots of articles that you can repurpose and upload quickly then this can be a good passive income stream that may only take a day or two to establish. Note also that Bukisa pay you a percentage of the commission made by anyone you refer, so another strategy if you have a large audience is to encourage them to join via your link. Many Bukisa members make this their main strategy as having a large number of people in your network on Bukisa can be a more efficient, more lucrative approach than writing and uploading hundreds or thousands of articles.

About.com

Apply to become an About.com guide and you will be required to submit sample articles and blog posts and, if accepted to stage two, set up a sample site on a specialist topic. If you get accepted you will be required to write regularly on your specialist topics, and perhaps create newsletters and moderate your community. There is a list of specialist topics available at any one time on the About.com site. Guides are paid a base amount per month plus incentives for page view growth. At the time of writing the basic payment starts at $500.

Suite101

With Suite101 you also write on specialist topics, and earn based on the popularity of your articles and their 'searchability' according to the site – basically you get an unspecified share of revenue from AdSense and banner ads. People need to click on the ads on the same page as your article for you to earn. You give Suite101 the exclusive right to your content for a year.

MAKING IT PAY

Once you have made a start earning money through writing online, I would advise you to be constantly on the lookout for more and better-paid work. Even if you have one regular client who gives you plenty of work, consider what might happen if that client decided they no longer needed you. There are plenty of reasons such as company cutbacks or changes in direction that can lead to freelance work being cut, so it pays to have a number of contracts on the go if possible.

What is more, if you are always open to new opportunities you will be able to build up your portfolio and develop your writing in a range of areas, topics or styles as almost every job differs. Again, this puts you in a stronger position when pitching for new work.

When you have a range of work coming in you may want to consider taking on better-paid work and dropping some of the less well-paid work. You may need to weigh up the benefits of, say, a reliable job that you do every month for a lower rate compared to a better-paid job that is less regular.

It is at this point that you might want to find others to write for you. As mentioned above, there are many people looking for online writing work as it can be done flexibly and from home. If you can bring in more than enough work you could consider taking on one or more writers and subcontracting work to them. You will need to check your contract and your client's expectations, but this can be a great way to move on from exchanging time for money.

Case Study: Carol Smith of New Mummy Tips and Professional Blogging Services

www.dancewithoutsleeping.co.uk

Carol Smith was a commercial assistant for a chilled food company, working on product launches and tracking sales trends. She wanted to work part-time after she became a mother, but was told she couldn't, so she resigned. She'd been blogging since her daughter was twelve weeks old, after 'meeting' people on Twitter who encouraged her to join British Mummy Bloggers (www.britmums.co.uk). She was offered a number of products for review so launched 'New Mummy's Tips', a blog purely for the purpose of reviews, money saving tips and advice. She says,

> I was struggling to find part time work, so when I was offered advertising for my blog I thought, 'Let's see if I can make some money online.' I then got offered paid work with a number of American blogs writing reviews at $20 each, and did some paid posts. I saw a video from Antonia and Erica about becoming a professional blogger. I set up a page, tweeted out my availability and since then have regular work helping businesses with their social media presence.

I did quite a lot of free writing to build up my presence which meant people knew and liked the way I write, and this led to a number of small jobs. I now help people with Twitter and Facebook, scheduling posts and devising social media plans. I have worked for one company, going through their site making it more 'people friendly', and then helped set up their Facebook fan page and Twitter account and devise a plan of giveaways, samples etc. My main role is now working with BecomeaMumpreneur.com, moderating their community and supporting their members as well as creating regular Twitter campaigns.

Carol still earns from her blogs. She says,

I have 20 parents on a review panel, with children from a few weeks old to 19. This has evolved into a new blog called Parent Panel.co.uk for reviews, while gift guides, days out and guest bloggers appear on New Mummy's Tips, which is now a lifestyle site for parents which brings in advertising revenue. I now have lots of contacts so can call in products for review when I need. I also run MakeItBakeIt.co.uk, a food and craft blog doing food reviews and recipes, with a great team of mum writers. Again, it brings in money from advertising. Some of the adverts pay per page view. I do not tend to take affiliates or click buys: I would rather have the space there for a direct ad that brings in £30 or £50 per month. I do use Amazon Affiliates when writing reviews. For New Mummy Tips I also take sponsored posts. For these review sites, 70% of my traffic comes from search engines, so I need to be smart with my titles and SEO, different to my personal blog where I can be funny. I am also working on a job board, findtherightperson.co.uk, which will link designers, bloggers and social media professionals to businesses needing their services. I'll make an income from small fees for job adverts and profiles, plus advertising and sponsors.

TAKE ACTION

If you want to write online to make money, get clear about your key skills. If you write in a niche where there is little competition you will be able to command better rates. Create a great show-case for your work: this could be your regular blog if you are simply looking for blog writing jobs, but a purpose-built blog site with testimonials, services and rates is usually best. Next, make as many contacts as possible aware of your services. Place profiles on sites like LinkedIn, send information about your services to contacts at relevant companies, and check out what you might earn if you go after jobs on freelancing websites. Plan time every week to pitch for new work as well as time doing the work itself.

11 From Promotion to Sales

I n a lot of ways, this is the most important chapter in this book, as we bring together everything you have learnt so far about building your reputation and creating your products, then help you learn the techniques that will actually make sales.

Selling is not straightforward: a lot of site owners operate on the 'build it and they will come' principle, but it can take more time, more promotion and more traffic than you might expect to create a great online income. Having said that, once you have everything set up and learn what works, you can apply your knowledge to new areas and swiftly build the multiple streams of income that will give you solid reliable earnings every month.

EMAIL: THE KEY TO SALES

Regular email communications are vital to driving sales. Why? Well, people who are 'warm' to you will buy more from you. Just think about how you feel when confronted with a cold call or an approach from a salesperson in a store. You are not in the mood, not interested, and want to end the interaction as soon as possible. But you will feel entirely differently if a good friend is chatting with you and happens to mention a great book that they have read, a fab film that they have seen or a product that they have bought and loved. You are much more likely to want to read the book, watch the film or buy the product. Through your emails to your list you need to become a virtual trusted friend, so people welcome, value and act on your recommendations.

Email communication is the culmination of a lot of your other online marketing and efforts to build your expert profile. Make it easy for everyone who is a Facebook fan, a Twitter follower or a blog reader to become a newsletter subscriber. Then, when you have the person's email, you can really develop the relationship you have started out there in the social media world. Make them feel part of an exclusive club whose members get all your best stuff. Sub-categorize your list so you meet people's needs and do not bombard them with unwanted mail. Offer them great exclusives and they will be loyal customers and look forward to your next email.

Case Study: Wendy Shand of Tots to Travel

www.totstotravel.co.uk

Wendy Shand runs holiday company 'Tots to Travel', providing safe and family friendly holiday homes for parents with small children. She uses Twitter, Facebook pages and a blog to draw in visitors and has changed her website over the years to make sure it is as effective as possible. Wendy explains how she has altered her expectations for the first contact with potential customers via the website:

It is about understanding what is the most wanted action from the front page of your site. My obvious answer was that I want people to buy a holiday, but that is not actually the right answer. If what you are selling has a value of more than £35–50 no-one will spend that much money before they know you, trust you and like you. I therefore need the chance to build a relationship with people, and am using the front page of the website to do this. I aim to build up my database of people who are interested in family holidays.

One of the best ways to do that is to write or provide something that people actually want, so they sign up for it and share their contact details with you. In my case I wrote a tips booklet on stress free family holidays. I wrote it myself. It didn't take that long. I mostly had the information at my fingertips and expanded information I had already. When you get down to it, these things do not take as long as you think.

Wendy now has the booklet on offer on the front page of the site and uses it to attract people to whom she can then send her regular email newsletter. She explains, 'From when people sign up, we are beginning to engage in a relationship. It might take 3–4 years before someone buys a holiday from us, and that's where the social media activities kick in. Our newsletter is not sell, sell, sell. It gives information and shares our values with clients and prospective clients.'

Wendy also has a video, logos and testimonials on the front page of her site. She says:

The video is really a way of giving business a personality. People buy from people they like and people they trust. Putting a face to the brand can feel uncomfortable in the beginning but is wholly necessary. We also add 'website bling' in terms of media logos to add credibility and reassurance that we are not a fly by night company. We are established and recognised by the press. Plus, we have lots of testimonials on the front page. We have social proof to reassure customers that we provide great customer services, and all the things that mums and dads need to book a family holiday.

By adapting her front page, Wendy has made improvements to her site statistics. She explains:

We have increased the home page conversion from less than 0.5% to 3.5% by adding the video and the free tips booklet. More importantly, what I have learnt is that marketing is not a one off thing. We are constantly tweaking different bits, measuring and retesting. We have a new video with improved quality to go up on the site. We have improved the message and hope to see an increase in home page conversion again.

Wendy also runs a site where she targets property owners: www.holidayhomerentalsite.com. She says:

We are working on this to include all the same elements as on the Tots to Travel site. One site should only be trying to do one thing. In having our message for property owners on the same site as for families booking holidays, the message can become muddled. We created a simple WordPress site that is more dynamic so it is picked up by search engines. Thinking about the lifetime value of a client, you understand how much you can spend on them to recruit them. With a holiday home owner, they have a lifetime of around 10 years with us, and could be 10 times more valuable to us than a one off holiday maker. We have a unique selling point for this group that parents with pre-schoolers often rent properties outside peak season. It made sense to set up a site specifically for this group.

Build your list

The first step to creating sales is to create a list. We are not talking about a 'to do' list, but a list of email addresses of people who have opted in to receive communications from you. Contact details of people who know what you are up to and are open to hearing from you are an incredibly valuable resource. To start building a list for yourself, you need an email service provider (ESP). An ESP provides you with a way to gather contacts and get in touch with them via email. It can cope when you have a handful of subscribers right up to when you have thousands of people on your list in a way that you wouldn't be able to manage via your own inbox. Using an ESP can help you comply with requirements to protect people's data and allow them to opt out of your emails. Here are some things to consider when choosing your ESP.

Finding the right ESP for you

Many ESPs offer free or low cost trials. Check out the ones on this list and see which looks right for you:

1. Constant Contact: www.constantcontact.com
2. Aweber: www.aweber.com
3. Vertical Response: www.VerticalResponse.com
4. MailChimp: www.mailchimp.com
5. Mad Mimi: www.madmimi.com
6. 1ShoppingCart: www.1shoppingcart.com
7. iContact www.icontact.com

How do different ESPs compare?

Test out the different autoresponders. They all vary, so weigh up the following factors:

1. Price
2. Delivery rates
3. Reliability

4. Ease of use

5. Support/customer service

Functions of email service providers

An ESP can do much more than just send emails. Not all ESPs offer all functions so have a think about which of these you need now ... and which might be vital as your business grows. Changing ESP can lead to you losing valuable contacts as people have to opt back in to receive communications from you, so take time to try out different options.

Available functions include:

- newsletter templates
- surveys
- shopping carts
- autoresponders
- digital product support

Creating a sign-up form

Once you have chosen your ESP you need to go to your ESP dashboard and create a sign-up form. Each ESP should have a guide on how to do this, and at the end of the process you will be given HTML code, which you can paste into a box in the sidebar of your website or blog. You can have several sign-up forms, which will all sign up leads to the same list: consider a sign-up box on your Facebook page, for example.

Driving traffic to your sign-up form

Once your sign-up form is live you need to drive traffic to it. You can do this in the following ways:

1. Writing blogs posts detailing your offer and embedding links to your sign-up form
2. Putting an advert in your blog/business website sidebar
3. Using Twitter, Facebook and other social media to drive leads to your sign-up form
4. Invite existing customers to sign up

Plan focused drives over a period of weeks or months to get people to sign up to your email list to find out about a particular launch or promotion. This is a great way to get people from your Facebook page, or Twitter followers, to take the next step and share their email address with you. Check whether your ESP offers an app to integrate your sign-up form with your Facebook page. Post on your page or tweet several times a week about your exciting upcoming promotion for newsletter subscribers only – you will find it gives your numbers a real boost.

Remember, though, that you want targeted followers on your sign-up list: people who are likely to find your products and services relevant to their needs. Offer a relevant incentive to sign up to find targeted traffic.

Sign-up incentives

Once you have chosen an ESP, decide what you will offer to those who sign up for your email list. In the past people may have signed up out of interest, but now you need to give them a powerful reason to sign up, something that offers so much value that they can't say no. Pick a bonus that targets your potential customer: parenting tips for toddlers if you sell products for the under threes, for example. This is the way to attract relevant people, also known as targeted traffic, who will find what you have to offer of interest.

Here are some ideas:

DISCOUNTS

Can your shopping cart take discount codes? Why not create a code for new sign-ups and, when people click to join your list, use an autoresponder to send them their code by return. Or can you create an exclusive page on your site that includes a half price offer? Again, use an autoresponder message to send new sign-ups to the page with the offer. Ensure that their link is time limited in some way so that they are incentivized to act fast. You can create attractive vouchers within some ESPs too. The advantage of creating a discount code is that right away you are drawing people further up your sales funnel and getting them into the buying habit. The disadvantage is that some people would rather get something free!

PRIZES

You could incentivize people with a prize for the 100th sign-up, the 500th sign-up and so on. Remember that you may need a fairly significant prize to make this work. Consider what prize would motivate your target audience, and ensure that you announce the winners on a regular basis to keep people motivated. If you develop an affiliate scheme (see Chapter 9) you could also offer prizes for top referrers.

eBOOKS AND eCOURSES

In the chapters on eBooks and eCourses we mentioned that these make great sign-up incentives. Your sign-up incentive needs to be something free that appeals to people who are likely to move on to purchase your paid products and a free report or course works well. If you are selling eCourses or eBooks, offering a free eCourse or eBook will attract people who like their information delivered in this way and will introduce eLearning to those unfamiliar with its concepts. Deliver excellent and compelling information in your sign-up bonus and build in automatic upsells to your paid product if you offer an eCourse and you will be well on your way to creating a marketing system that sells your products for you.

WEBINARS AND TELECLASSES

A webinar or teleclass is a great way to build your list. A webinar is like an online presentation with sound and images while a teleclass uses sound only. You will need to sign up for a teleclass provider and an autoresponder: most providers will give attendees the option of listening online or via a telephone number. Create a sign-up page on your site, with an autoresponder message that includes details of how to sign up for the teleclass or webinar. Pick a topic that you are an expert on, or choose an expert to interview who will appeal to people who might buy your products. Then, publicize the opportunity using your current contacts and social media.

Providers

There are lots of teleclass and webinar providers. Some offer free services, but with a limited number of class attendees. Others, like GoToWebinar, offer options for hundreds or thousands of attendees, depending on the fee you pay. You might also want the facility to record your classes so that you can offer them as a sign-up incentive on an ongoing basis or add them to the range of products you sell.

Now that you have plenty of ideas about how to attract people to your list, create a plan so that you can try different ones for a month or two. See what works well for you and remember that having a range of time limited offers throughout the year can really maximize the growth of your list. Many people won't bother to sign up for something, even if it is free. Point out the benefits and value, and explain that they only have a very limited time to get the freebie and you will find that far more people take action.

Creating your communications

Your next step is to create a regular programme of communications. Do not sit down and start writing a single newsletter: do create a plan of what you are going to market throughout the year and then plan your communications to support this. Many companies opt for a newsletter style communication with a blend of feature articles, news and promotions. This model is a good way to drive traffic to your business website and interest customers, but it is often too chatty to drive sales. If you have time, schedule in this sort of newsletter to fill in gaps between active campaigns and remind your list of all the expert help you offer.

More importantly, devise campaigns with short clear direct emails with a single message as this is the best way to increase sales. According to *Email Marketing: An Hour a Day,* an email subscriber will purchase 167% more than a non email subscriber, but they still need a clear call to action, like 'buy now'. People will only buy if you give them a clear message: what single action would you like people to take based on the email?

Ideally use a time limited offer too. 'Time limiting' your offers is critical to getting people to take action: read on to find out more about motivating your readers to take the next step.

What results do you want to achieve?

When creating your marketing plan, you need to be clear about your targets for each promotion. Do you want to sell ten courses or a hundred eBooks or sign up fifty new subscribers after a particular campaign? If you know what result you want you can focus all your communications, sales pages etc. to achieve that aim.

Relationship building

Alongside planning your products and creating a marketing campaign, you should also invest time in understanding your followers and what makes them tick. As you develop a better understanding of their thought processes you will be better able to create marketing that is relevant to them and gives you good results. Here are some ideas to get you started:

Showcase your expertise

In Chapter 3 we looked at building your profile as an expert. This helps enormously when you are moving into the sales phase. Once people have come across you in the position of 'expert', they will perceive you in a different way and be more likely to purchase from you. Consider who *you* perceive to be an expert that you look up to. What qualities in that person do you respect? How do they communicate? What could you learn from them when positioning yourself as an expert? Go back and review Chapter 3 if you need more ideas about raising your profile as an expert.

Build trust

Once you have started to build your expert profile, you also need to consider how you are building trust. Look at others you trust: what do they do that builds your trust? Who do you buy from, and how do you feel when, say, you share your credit card number over their site? What makes you feel sufficient trust to do this?

There are a number of ways to build trust. Start by giving without asking for something in return. Be generous with great content. Be consistent: post on your blog on a regular basis, have your branding throughout your sites, email communications, social media accounts and shopping cart. Do things when you say that you will. Be authentic: if you are true to your own values in all your communications people are more likely to trust you and you will find it easier to be consistent.

When selling something, offer a guarantee. People are more likely to purchase if they know that they can send something back with no questions asked, for example. You can make the most of being affiliated to payments gateways like PayPal, Mastercard or Visa by displaying their logos at the point of payment. Plus, you can highlight other ways that you keep people's information safe and link to your privacy policy if you are asking them to share their contact details.

Create a sense of need

As well as creating trust, you also need to create a sense of need. Why should people desire your products? If you look at marketing as a whole, businesses are selling the sizzle not the sausage. In other words, it is all about promoting the end result, the desirable state of mind or lifestyle rather than the actual product. Buy this and you will be happy, more beautiful, and more attractive: that's the message behind all the adverts with beautiful people in glamorous locations, 'living the dream'. This technique is used in magazines, on television and on websites too. This is where your choice of site design and illustrations for your sales page can make a great difference as well as the words you use.

Write about the benefits of the products or services you offer rather than describing the features. Think about how they will help your customer achieve their dream. Describe the feelings that they will have once they have used the product or service.

As part of this, you need to understand what problems there are in your target audience's lives, and you need to focus your products on solving them. Review the sections on market research if you are unclear about the problems your customers have.

Motivate people

Once you have built trust, created a sense of need and sold the benefits, you need to get your followers to focus their attention on what you are selling. Here is one way to do this.

Scarcity makes something more desirable: that's why internet marketers limit the number of packages or products available. Consider your own feelings when you are after a product on an eBay auction and there is only one available. You might bid more or click 'buy it now', whereas if there is a listing with forty-seven products available, or lots of similar objects on offer from different sellers, you will be more likely to only bid up to a lower limit, safe in the knowledge that you can try again another day if you do not win that auction. Can you apply this to your products too? You may feel that you are imposing an artificial limit but scarcity will allow you to charge more.

Urgency will also drive people to take action. You will make far fewer sales of items with ongoing availability than those that are available for a limited time. Offer flash sales for twenty-four hours or three days only, and send a couple of emails to announce the start and end, plus an extra motivating email in the middle of a three-day sale. Open the sign-up for eCourses for one week only, with plenty of advanced warning to motivate people to note the opening date, and send emails during the week to explain all the reasons to take part and remind your subscribers that they only have a short time to participate. From a marketing point of view you can then send people a 'last chance to buy' email, which will drive all those who have been considering a purchase to take action.

Use the 'scarcity' and 'urgency' motivators as part of your marketing plan: you can then bring back popular products later in the year and tell people how they sold out in thirty-six hours, for example, demonstrating further the popularity of what you offer and the need to act fast.

Twitter is a great place to provide countdowns of the number of days and hours until an offer closes, or the limited number of products available. You can also install a countdown ticker on your sales page.

TAKING PAYMENTS

Critical to this whole process of making money online, you need a straightforward way to take payments from your customers. For the majority of online businesses, automatic payment systems are important so that your customer can click a button to buy rather than you having to send payment requests or invoices. The first place to start when you are in the early stages of growing an online business is to sign up with PayPal. PayPal allows you to create buttons, accept credit cards and receive online payments for one-off amounts and subscriptions. It is simple to operate and well recognized in the online world. Note that it is not available in all countries in the world, but does serve a good proportion. You pay a percentage of each fee received to PayPal and can upgrade your PayPal account for a fee each month, which gives you access to services such as taking credit cards over the phone. PayPal withdrawals to your bank account take 3–5 working days.

PayPal does have limits on the amount of money that you can receive to an unverified account before it requires further checks: check the limits and verify the status of your account before you do any big launches.

Looking beyond PayPal, you may want to set up a merchant account, which allows you to take credit and debit card payments. If you have a business bank account, ask the bank manager or helpline about setting up a merchant account. This can be straightforward, or it may take several months if you haven't been trading for long.

A business gateway, such as Sagepay or RBS WorldPay, is the secure website that processes the credit cards for you and then passes on the money to you. These allow you to process money without having to set up your own site with secure certification. You can simply apply for a business gateway on its own, or get a merchant account too.

Compare different deals: you will be paying a few per cent

commission plus a monthly fee if you take credit cards via a merchant account and business gateway. Also, think about which currencies you want to take: for most online business it is wise to be able to take US dollars. Business gateways hang on to your money for a certain period in case of queries on payments, which you should take into account when planning your cash flow forecast.

Do allow several months for setting up your payment systems if you want to use anything beyond PayPal, and particularly if you are setting up a new business. Even PayPal cheques can take a few days. If you are a member of a business organization you may get a good deal on a merchant account by going via the organization.

If you are new to online business or focusing simply on information products, PayPal is certainly the easiest and fastest option. A significant proportion of online businesses stick with PayPal and need nothing more. Check out the different options available to you and see which suits your business.

HOW TO CREATE AND STRUCTURE YOUR CONTENT

Now you are all set up to start selling. Here are some key features to include in your website or email copy when you are actively trying to bring in sales. If you are creating a long sales page you may use all of these features. For your newsletter or emails in the run-up to a launch you might slot in a mix of testimonials and fact-based articles. Think about what is right for your audience.

Headline

Your headline is critical to the success of any communication. Get it right and you will interest people from the start. Get it wrong and you will lose them before they have even read the rest of your carefully crafted copy. Consider the key issue you are addressing with your product as that might inspire your headline.

Sometimes you can use shock headlines, perhaps with a double meaning:

- Bad News! – a title for an email where you reveal that you have something in limited supply only
- Going Under! – a title that could draw people's attention and concern

Use headlines that show social proof:

- Everyone should know about this – do you?
- Who else wants to...?
- I know five millionaires who have subscribed to...

Focus on how your products solve problems:

- Are you struggling with...?
- Three quick ways to beat...
- Do you make this mistake time after time?

Imply insider knowledge:

- The secret to...
- The quick and easy way to...
- Little known ways to...
- See how easily you could...

Keep headlines short: aim for 30–40 characters. Do not be too cryptic as cryptic can easily be confusing!

Feelings

Consider your readers' feelings and emotions. If you can write in a way that evokes good feelings, you are on to a winner. Video communications can be powerful ways to create good content and with some email newsletter providers you can now embed videos, as well as having them on your site. If using video, ensure that you make the most of words, images and music too.

One systematic way to look at the feelings you need to evoke to make a sale comes in the form of the marketing acronym AIDA.

Start by getting people's attention with a focused headline plus key details in the first few lines that really sell how good your product or service will make someone *feel*.

Create interest by highlighting your offering's strongest problem-solving aspects and key benefits. You might find a case study is a good way to interest people: people like stories. *Or* a video about your own experience might interest people. At this point you could also pique interest by pointing out that something is popular, limited in number or only available for a short time.

The third stage is creating desire for the product, persuading the person that they need and want what is on offer. It is often said that consumers do not buy products, they buy benefits or desired results. Let your audience know exactly what these are. If you have used the product yourself then you can give your reader your unique insights into this. If you are selling a weight loss programme or a business success programme, show how you or someone who has used the programme is now slim and desirable or wealthy and desirable.

As an alternative at this point, instead of going straight to desire you could look at *description*, followed by points to *persuade* people and testimonials to add *proof*.

The fourth and final action is to encourage your reader to take action, in this case to make a purchase. This can be done through a direct call to action such as 'buy X now' and also highlighting any time limits or scarcity, for example, if there are only X amount of products available.

Testimonials

Testimonials are critical to building trust, as mentioned earlier in this book. Make sure that you call up some of your current customers or clients and ask them these three questions, adapted to your own offer. This will help you devise a powerful testimonial.

- What was your situation before you used this product/took this course?
- What was your experience using it?
- What difference has it made to your life/your business?

For a great testimonial you want to demonstrate a journey to a better place. Ask people for facts and figures: did they save £50, lose 20 lbs or generate an income of £1,000?

Facts

When writing a long sales page, one of your aims may be to answer all the questions that people have about your offer. Here are some ideas from a sales page we have used. We used these questions as headlines and provided a paragraph below each with the answers. Insert the name of your product or course and see what answers you might come up with. The idea is to prove the value of what you are offering before coming to the final question which explains the price:

- When is [the course]?
- Who is [the course] for?
- Where is [the course]?
- What if I have already started [another course]?
- What is covered in [the course]?
- So how much is [the course]?

Demonstrating value

As part of your sales copy you need to demonstrate the value of what you offer. As well as the testimonials and persuasive copy or video highlighting benefits, it can be useful to actually add up in monetary terms everything that people get when they join a course, for example. You may consider adding in bonus material at a launch as many people are persuaded by the extra value of a bonus or two. Think about other ways to prove that people are getting enormous value for a relatively small investment.

Price or no price?

Some people do include a price on their sales page or in their newsletter, some do not. Think about the message you are putting across, whichever way you decide to go. If you do not mention the price some people may click through just to see how much it costs, while others will click to buy as they haven't been deterred by seeing the actual cost: once you have made them click that button you have them one step closer to completing the sale.

Alternatively, you may feel that it is important to be upfront about both the tremendous value you offer and the price of the course. If you can demonstrate that the value far outweighs the cost you are well on your way to persuading people to buy.

Calls to action and purchase buttons

At this point, we should address calls to action once more. This has been mentioned throughout the book, but telling people what to do next is vital to the success of any online marketing. Tell people that they want what you are offering, and some will believe you. Show them that others have loved your stuff, and more will be convinced. Persuade them that you can solve a problem that is relevant to them, leaving them happier, healthier or wealthier and you are on your way to creating desire. Then say, 'Buy Now' or 'Click here to join', or 'Become a Success' and you will have made the sale.

Study calls to action that you see on- and offline. Consider the action that you want people to take, and create a short phrase that sums it up.

Perry Belcher has studied the different aspects of persuading people to make that final click and has designed a well thought out 'buying area' button. It uses a range of elements including a box to make the button stand out, colours that encourage people to take action and payment logos to increase trust. Find out more and watch the video at www.belcherbutton.com

Repetition

When writing a long sales page or creating a series of emails, repeat information so people do not have to click back. Never assume that people will remember or retain information: always make it as easy as possible to take action. This is particularly relevant when you have a long sales page and need several calls to action at different points. Put crucial text at the beginning and end of any page or letter as these are the parts people recall the most.

Follow-up page if people click away

Finally, look at your shopping cart or payment gateway and see if you can set up a link to refer people on to a page if they click to purchase but then change their minds. In this you can have a list of compelling reasons to take action, an extra bonus or even a survey to find out why they clicked away.

Case Study: Karen Skidmore of CanDoCanBe

www.candocanbe.com

I started off in business in 2004. Starting out in business back then, you needed a business card, you needed letterheads, you needed a website, and you needed a leaflet: the classic marketing kit. When I realised that classic marketing kit wasn't working for me, that's when I started looking at the website. Back in 2004–5 people were moving from a traditional five page website to something that was more interactive. The web was just starting to evolve. Blogging was starting to be born and email newsletters were starting. Just having a website on the internet didn't do you any good: people went and had a look at your website and that's as far as it went. I was thinking: 'What I am doing to get life coaching clients is not working and I am not making money.'

I had to start building a database. That's when I got into email newsletters. I knew I had to get people on to a system so I could market to them. I did this on a monthly basis to start with and it has progressed over years. Once I realised that, that's when I started thinking how am I going to use the website to get people to subscribe to the email newsletter. And then I got into blogging. I met a very knowledgeable chap called Graham Jones, an internet psychologist, who told me what the blog is and how it works. Suddenly a whole new world opened up. I started to realise what blogging could do for a business: creating content, being able to showcase yourself without selling yourself all the time, you are actually sharing information.

So that's when the blog got bolted onto my marketing and that's where social media has come in too, in recent years. I began to understand that Twitter, Facebook and

LinkedIn all could be ways to get people onto my website to add themselves to my email newsletter list.

You do not have to enjoy writing but if you have stories to tell about what you did and your business a blog is instrumental in giving you a place to share your knowledge and showcase your expertise, what you do with your customers and what you sell online. I couldn't do what I do without the blog.

And the other thing is email newsletters. I was in a meeting last week with a big company and the web marketing manager was saying email marketing is dying: I disagree and think it is the backbone of business sales. We are spending more time on Facebook and Twitter, but email marketing is critical in bringing it all together and building long term relationships with people and being able to sell to them at the same time. You are forming passing relationships with people on Twitter: try and sell too much and people won't take notice of your tweets or will stop following you. It is about bringing people to the point of saying 'I am interested in being a customer with you at some point in the future, I do not necessarily want to buy from you right now but I trust you enough to share my name and email address with you'. And that's where you do the selling.

TAKE ACTION

Now you have come to the end of the book. Have you been working on projects as you have read, or are you about to take a big step forward into the unknown? Either way, now is the time to create an action plan.

Focus on your life goals first: think about what you want to achieve, and what success means to you. Make sure your plans to make money online tie in to these goals so you stay motivated. Then, scope out your products and services. Do your market research and create plans to build a list via your blog, Twitter, Facebook and the other means listed in this book. Think about what incentive you will offer to people joining your list.

Create trial products to gather your first testimonials and plan your marketing campaigns. Decide what outcome you want from each communication: if you are offering something for sale, does it come with something exclusive, at a discount, limited, extra? Plan your dates for launches: make each promotion a pressing matter – short deadlines create more incentive to act right away. Once you have your plans in place, start putting them into action right away!

Index